Live, Love, Fuck Off

A Memoir, A Meltdown,
A Main Character Era

Carrie Stovall

This book contains real experiences, colorful language, and unapologetic truths pulled straight from my real, raw, and occasionally ridiculous life. The stories are told as I remember them. Which means they've been filtered through memory, emotion, healing, humor, and possibly a few glasses of wine. Or rage. Or both.

Events and conversations are true to the best of my recollection, though timelines may blur and details may shift, because memory is a tricky little bitch (especially when fueled by caffeine, trauma, or petty grievances from 2009). Some names and identifying details have been changed to protect the guilty (or because I simply forgot who the hell they were). Sorry, not sorry. Feeling seen? Good. Now go talk about it in therapy.

This is not a how-to manual. It's not a memoir written under oath. It's a collection of truths; mine. Lived, learned, processed (admittedly oftentimes poorly), and retold with the full audacity of someone who's earned the right to say, *this happened to me.*

Legal stuff: The content herein is for entertainment, empowerment, and maybe a little emotional validation. It's not therapy. It's not medical advice. If you're experiencing anything heavy, life-altering, or soul-shaking, please seek professional help. I'm funny, but I'm not licensed.

Basically: these are my stories, my messes, my lessons, and my middle fingers. Read accordingly.

For my mom –

Who never stopped believing in me.
Even when I was too tired, too lost, or too loud.
Who loved me through every mess, meltdown, and moment
when I swore I had it all figured out.
Who gave me her strength, her sarcasm, and her stubborn heart.

This book is for you.

Contents

Introduction

Live, Love, Fuck Off: *A Memoir, A Meltdown, A Main Character Era*

Let me just get this out of the way: this isn't your typical self-help book. There will be no "ten steps to a better you," no softly-lit guru whispering about daily affirmations, and definitely no rise-and-grind nonsense (unless it's to pee at 5 a.m., stub your toe, and crawl back under the covers). If you came here for perfect answers, clean timelines, or anything resembling subtlety...buckle up, babe. You might have picked up the wrong book.

This book is a love letter to the beautiful disasters. The overthinkers. The people who feel everything too deeply and pretend to be fine until they absolutely *are not*. It's a memoir stitched together with meltdowns, milestones, and middle fingers. Think of it as the group chat message you didn't know you needed. With less filters and more fucks.

It's about life: real, raw, unfiltered life. The kind that throws grief and joy at you in the same week. The kind that leaves you sobbing in a parking lot one minute and laughing so hard you pee your pants a little the next. It's about the things we whisper to ourselves in the mirror, the trauma we've learned to joke about just to survive, the ex we should've ghosted six months earlier, and the family drama that would make excellent television if it weren't so personal.

This is for the woman who's been told she's too much, too emotional, too opinionated, too *anything*. The one who's stayed in situations that dimmed her light. The one who bends and breaks and still finds a way to rise with grace...and sarcasm. It's for the tired but still standing, the healing but still hurting, the fabulous but occasionally feral.

Each chapter pulls from the chaos of my own journey - childhood confusion, body image battles, sisterhood sagas, romantic detours, and breakthroughs I wish would have come with a warning label. I've walked through fire, danced in the ashes, and rebuilt my damn self more times than I can count. I didn't come out unscathed, but I came out real, and out loud.

I wrote this the way I live my life:

With humor. With brutal honesty. With dramatic flair and an unapologetic heart.

Because healing doesn't have to be sterile or soft-spoken. Sometimes it's messy. Sometimes it's loud. And sometimes it looks a whole lot like telling the truth with glitter on your eyelids and a margarita in your hand.

So, pour a drink. Light a candle. Throw on your coziest hoodie or boldest red lip. Cry if you need to. Laugh like nobody's judging. And most importantly, don't you dare shrink for someone else's comfort. You didn't survive everything you've been through just to become palatable.

This is your permission slip to live louder.

Love harder.

And when necessary…

Tell them to fuck right off.

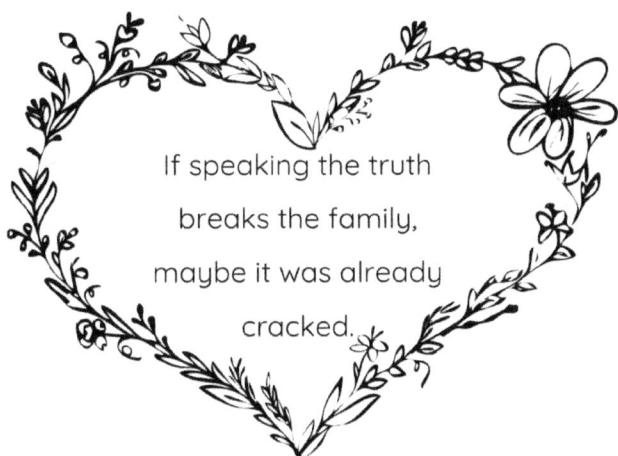

If speaking the truth
breaks the family,
maybe it was already
cracked.

Chapter 1:
Did I Break the Family or Nah?

Turns out, telling the truth makes you the villain when the family loves a good lie.

I was raised on the idea that *family is everything.* And I believed it, deep down in my little dysfunctional heart, like gospel whispered through gritted teeth.

My mom's side of the family praised themselves constantly. If you listened to them talk long enough, you'd think we were the gold standard of generational success. Always a new photo op. Always some weird flex about how "close-knit" we were. Meanwhile, my dad's side? Quiet, but chaotic, slightly feral, and oddly warm in that "pass the trauma with the gravy" kind of way. Family dysfunction didn't hide behind polite smiles; it wore flip-flops and said the quiet part out loud.

Inside our actual household, things were...complicated. We loved each other, sure. But it was the kind of love that came with an edge. Love that slammed doors. That left things unsaid for decades. That sometimes looked more like survival than support. But still, I called it home. I called it family.

After growing up in the middle of all that, I became the default. The emotional translator. The peacemaker. The one who got the phone calls when someone stormed out, or someone else needed fixing. No one *gave* me the cape. I just picked it up and started wearing it. Because if I didn't, who would?

My parents split when I was young, which meant weekends with Dad. My stepsisters were like bonus rounds in a life I never really got to settle into. But the soundtrack of those visits? Always the same.

Him and my stepmom, tag-teaming their bitterness, turning casual conversations into low-budget smear campaigns against my mom.

"She doesn't take good enough care of the girls."
"She's always traveling."
"She uses all the child support on herself."
"Speaking of, that child support is draining us."

And my favorite one of all that was *quite literally* said from childhood well into adulthood…

"I can't believe she still had her Christmas tree up in February."

They said these things with the confidence of people who forgot there were children in the room. But I was always listening. We all were. And every one of those words dripped like poison into the cracks of my foundation. Cracks that would later shape my doubts, my fears, my inner voice that didn't always sound like my own.

As an adult, I can see the split so clearly now.

My mom? She owned it. Every hard conversation, every failure, every time she fell short. She has looked me in the eye and said, "You're right. I'm sorry. I didn't know how to be better then, but I'm trying now."

That kind of humility? That kind of growth? That's rare. That's sacred. That's why I'll be annoying about my mom forever. If I talk about her like she's the damn queen of redemption, it's because she earned the title.

Now my dad? He just…keeps moving. No acknowledgment. No accountability. No real conversations. Just a man stuck in a loop of old narratives and quiet avoidance. We don't talk about the past because to him it's already over, and to revisit it would mean admitting there was something to fix. I used to wait for that call. That moment. That apology. But I've learned to stop holding my breath. It's exhausting trying to heal a wound someone else won't even admit they caused.

When my marriage ended, I blamed myself. And honestly? I still do, sometimes. I spent 11 years loving a man who couldn't love himself. Who mistook my softness for stupidity. Who, when it ended, scorched my name in rooms I'd never even entered. I'm done carrying shame that isn't mine, though. If dragging me helps someone sleep at night, I hope they dream well.

I've spent years holding space for other people's healing like a damn emotional sherpa. Always being the one who got the "Can you just talk to them?" texts, even when *I* was the one bleeding out.

Even with all the chaos, I never expected the real break to come from the person closest to me. My sister. The one I thought would be there forever. It wasn't a blowout or some explosive betrayal, it was quieter than that. But somehow, silence hit harder than screams. I'll get into all of that later. Just know: when your built-in person suddenly isn't, it shakes something deep in your bones.

The last real conversation I had with her ended something like this:

"Make it better. You're the only one people listen to."

I didn't even know what I was supposed to fix. I still to this day don't even fully realize what happened. But somehow, it landed on me. Again. That was the moment I realized: I can't keep setting myself on fire to keep everyone else warm.

I've stood up when it counted. I've spoken out when silence felt like betrayal. Once, I defended someone in our family. Called out something we all *knew* was wrong. And what did it get me? A blistering text thread. A screaming match. An aunt I *adored* telling me to "crawl back under your rock."

I didn't break the family. The family was already cracked. I just stopped pretending the pieces still fit.

I've been the scapegoat. The glue. The emotional dump truck. I've been guilted, ghosted, and gaslit into submission. But here's what I know now:

Love with conditions? That's not love.

Silence in the face of harm? That's not loyalty.

Being the glue? Only works if the other pieces *want* to be whole.

These days, I don't care if people listen to me. I care that I'm telling the truth. Loudly. Unapologetically. And if that truth makes someone uncomfortable?

They were probably too comfortable in the lie.

For Anyone Who's the "Family Glue" That's Tired of Sticking Shit Together

If you've ever been the one expected to keep the peace, fix the rift, and absorb the emotional damage, this is your permission slip to stop. You are not responsible for managing other people's chaos at the cost of your own peace.

You are allowed to set boundaries, tell your truth, and love people from a distance. You can mourn what never was and still build something stronger for yourself. You deserve love that feels like freedom, not obligation.

Let them call you cold. Let them say you've changed. Let them whisper that you're the reason whatever happened, happened. Because guess what? You're not an emotional janitor hired to clean up after everyone's messes.

You're not selfish for saying, "Not my problem," when people keep tossing their baggage at your feet like it's lost luggage. At some point, carrying the weight of everyone else's dysfunction turns into a full-body injury. And babe, you're not going out like that.

So, here's your new role: Chief Executive Officer of Your Own Damn Peace. You get to choose who sits at your table, who gets a front-row seat, and who can love you without strings attached. Being the "family glue" only works when you don't lose yourself in the process. You're allowed to leave the broken pieces on the floor and say, "Actually? I'm not fixing that."

Because protecting your peace isn't betrayal, it's *survival.*

My love language?
Not being constantly emotionally
hijacked - who knew?

Chapter 2:

Raised by Chaos, Married by Mayhem

When dysfunction is your normal, love looks a lot like survival.

I grew up in noise.

Anger wasn't just a mood; it was the language.

My mom came from a big, loud Italian family where yelling was the love language and silence meant someone had either died or was plotting revenge. Her father shouted like it paid the bills. Her mother? She mastered the art of pretending not to hear it. It wasn't just accepted, it was *expected*.

I don't remember much about my parents being married, they divorced when I was two, but I remember everything that came after. Both remarried. My stepdad was a storm disguised as a man. He and my oldest sister fought like it was their job, and when she wasn't at war with him, she was going head-to-head with our other sister. My younger sister and me? We clung to each other like lifeboats; two kids trying to find a quiet corner in a house that never knew peace.

When I wasn't at home, I was at my aunt's house. Which was...great? If you enjoy tension so thick it hums. Her husband didn't have a volume setting under 10, and violent outbursts were just part of the soundtrack. My cousin and I were basically trauma-bonded by age seven.

Eventually, my mom and stepdad split. My sisters bolted the second they could, and that left just me and Mom. We did our best in the quiet that followed, but quiet doesn't mean peaceful when your nervous system is still running fire drills from the past.

I'd love to say it got better as I got older. But trauma has a twisted sense of humor…and a habit of picking your partners.

At 18, I landed in a textbook abusive relationship. He was much older, had two kids (one with special needs) and a family that believed he walked on water. I gave him everything I had (which, at eighteen, wasn't a lot). In return? I got control, manipulation, and violence dressed up as passion. I was choked until I passed out. Hit in the face while driving. Beaten with an iron. And that's just what I'm willing to say out loud.

The physical wounds faded, but the emotional damage lingered like smoke in a house that had already burned down. One day, I finally looked in the mirror and realized: this isn't love. It never was. And I couldn't survive it one more day.

With my absolute saint of a mother's help, I planned my escape like I was a spy on a mission, while the kids were with their mother. I had *five minutes,* while he was gone, to grab what I could and get out. I left *everything* behind. And listen, I knew I could eventually replace all the clothing and furniture…but I still think about that damn Pampered Chef potato cutter I had. I swear that thing cut potatoes into the best French fries of my life.

Prepare yourselves because I'm not sure you're ready for the plot twist that came next…

His babies' mother, who was a *midnight ballerina* (thank you TikTok for coining that term) and could barely take care of herself, showed up on my doorstep with their youngest daughter. She was there begging me to take care of her. Because I loved and missed that child so much, I took her. And for the next two years she lived with me, and I co-parented with my abuser *and* his ex.

Read that again.

Because trauma will have you doing emotional gymnastics and sell it to you as stability.

This shared custody, *with no legal rights*, ended the day my sweet baby girl came back with bruises. I called her father to ask questions he didn't want to answer. The next thing I knew, her aunt and the police were at my door. That was the last time I saw the little girl who called me Mom.

What followed? A blur of relationships. Just enough to leave me dizzy, jaded, and painfully fluent in red flags.

Then I met *him*. My future husband. At a nightclub. There were immediate signs that told me I should've exited stage left. But no, I apparently love nightmares dressed as fairy tales. He came with a baby and a complicated past. That first year? A disaster, with a side of joint custody chaos. Even with all the mess of that first year, we held on tight and were married six months later. Fast, ugly, and intense. But that's a whole other chapter. Literally. We'll unpack that beautiful disaster in Chapter 10.

When you grow up in chaos, it starts to feel like home. Dysfunction becomes your comfort zone. So, when love walks in loud, dramatic, and exhausting, you don't run. You grab a seat, pour a drink, and call it normal. You start confusing adrenaline for chemistry, walking on eggshells for passion, and emotional whiplash for connection. Because the noise is familiar. And familiar feels safe, even when it's quietly destroying you.

But here's the thing: real love isn't supposed to feel like survival. It's not supposed to spike your cortisol or leave you constantly decoding someone else's moods like a human Ouija board. Real love doesn't leave you drained, dizzy, or second-guessing your worth.

It took years, therapy, and the dramatic loss of a very aggressive potato cutter, to realize that love doesn't have to hurt to be real. I don't need to earn it by sacrificing my sanity. I don't need to brace myself every time they walk into the room. I deserve the kind of love that's steady. Quiet in the best way. The kind that doesn't yell, doesn't throw, and sure as hell doesn't turn my nervous system into a war zone.

For Anyone Who Mistook Chaos for Connection

If your love life has felt more like a series of survival drills than a safe space, you're not alone. When dysfunction is your foundation, it makes peace feel suspicious. But love isn't supposed to be loud and painful. It's supposed to feel like *relief*. Healing means learning to stop chasing adrenaline and start choosing peace. You deserve the kind of love that doesn't leave bruises - physical, emotional, or otherwise.

Please understand that it is not your fault if chaos once felt like chemistry. If you confused red flags with butterflies, that's because no one taught you that real love doesn't make you anxious. It doesn't keep you guessing, apologizing, or shrinking yourself to be more appetizing. That gut feeling that something's off? Listen to it. That exhaustion after every conversation? Pay attention. Love isn't meant to drain you, it's meant to pour into you, not *out* of you.

If you're in a season of relearning what love *should* feel like, give yourself grace. The peace might feel boring at first. The calm might feel like silence. But keep going. One day, your nervous system will stop confusing quiet for danger. And that's when you'll know you've made it to the other side. The kind of love you're rebuilding now doesn't ask you to survive it. It asks you to rest in it.

Red hair, red flags,
red hot rage...
I contain multitudes.

Chapter 3:
Ginger Snapped

Red hair, relentless teasing, and a masterclass in growing thick skin.

Growing up a ginger in a world that treated me like some kind of mythical creature was…exhausting. I wasn't just the only redhead in my class; I was one of the only ones in the entire school. It felt like being dropped into a sitcom where I was the punchline and the writers really leaned into the hair jokes. And listen, kids are not known for their originality or their kindness. If one called me "carrot top," the next ten just ran with it like they'd invented the insult. I heard every version: Little Orphan Annie. Fire Crotch. Red-headed stepchild. As if being different was some kind of crime punishable by mockery.

When you're young, all you want is to blend in just enough to feel safe. To be invisible just long enough to catch your breath. But when your hair glows like a traffic cone under fluorescent lights, invisibility isn't on the menu. You learn early that you're going to stand out whether you like it or not. And eventually, you have to choose: either shrink and apologize for existing or lean into the fact that you're never going to disappear, so you might as well make it worth watching.

In elementary school, I had a secret weapon: my mom worked in the main office. That gave me just enough cool points to survive. I could sneak to her office for snacks, comfort, or just a break from the chaos. It was like having a mini escape hatch built into the building. I'd act like I was on some important mission, "just dropping off a paper", when really, I just needed five minutes of not being weird, not being teased, not being *on*. That place smelled like coffee, copy paper, and safety.

Middle school also threw me a bone; I was a cheerleader (yes, go ahead and picture it: full pep, loud voice, glitter bows). That squad gave me a little social armor. Uniforms, routines, and forced friendships will do that. Plus, doesn't everyone need someone to trust will catch you when you're thrown into the air? Turns out, shared risk builds a bond. Or at least a temporary ceasefire from bullying.

But high school? High school was the drop-off point where the safety net vanished. My older sister had chosen a different school, so naturally, I followed her and her friends to this new place…where I knew no one and absolutely did not belong. She and I weren't close then. Honestly, she and her crew had started calling me "Chucky" back in middle school. Not the cute kind. The horror movie icon with rage in his eyes and murder in his heart. I'd laugh along when they said it, because what else was I supposed to do? Cry? Not in front of the people already looking for my weakness. Survival meant making it a joke before anyone else could.

And if high school wasn't awkward enough, let's layer on our family dynamics for good measure. Another sister (ironically, the one I felt closest to) used to sing a little made-up song that included the phrase "carrot-topped n-word." I was a kid. She was my sister. And yes, I knew it was wrong, even then. But when cruelty comes from someone you love, it leaves a different kind of scar. A quieter one. A deeper one. It tells you that your pain isn't valid, not even at home. That the place where you're supposed to be safe is just another arena you have to survive.

These days, people pay big money to dye their hair the exact shade I used to pray would disappear. They call it rare. Beautiful. Fiery. They want to bottle it up and tag it on Instagram. But back then? Being rare meant being alone. And beauty? Not when you're being mocked for it every damn day. There was zero pride in it. Only discomfort and wishing to trade it in for something easier.

Still though, I'm here. Ginger, grown, and not letting anyone rewrite my story. The things I was teased for are now the things I treasure. I didn't just survive it all, I outlasted the noise. And now? That glow they made fun of? It's my damn spotlight.

For Anyone Who Was Bullied for Just *Being* Themselves

Being teased for something you can't control changes how you see yourself. But surviving it? That's where the power comes in. I used to think my red hair made me a target. Now I see it made me *tough*. If you've ever been picked on for being different, hear this: you were never the problem. The world just hadn't caught up to your magic yet. Keep standing out. Keep being bold. And don't you dare shrink to make other people comfortable.

Let them talk. Let them mock what they don't understand. Because what once made you a target is now your superpower. The ones who tried to dim your light were never ready for how bright you were. And maybe they still aren't. But that's not your burden to carry. You don't owe anyone an explanation for your shine. Not now, not ever.

You didn't just survive the bullying, you evolved. You built armor out of every insult, every side-eye, every whisper behind your back. And now? That armor's glittered with self-worth. So go ahead and wear your weird like a crown. Dye your hair neon pink, laugh too loud, take up all the space. The people who once made you feel too much? They were never *enough* to handle someone like you.

They said I was the strong one.
They meant the one they
emotionally dump on for free.

Chapter 4:
Cape, Crown, and Crippling Pressure

Being the strong one is cute…until it starts killing you.

I didn't wake up one day and decide, "You know what? I think I'll become the emotional backbone of this entire family."

But somehow, that's exactly what happened. No application. No orientation. Just a slow burn of expectations, quiet nods of approval, and the unspoken understanding that if *someone* was going to manage this family, it was going to be me.

Somewhere between being dependable and peacekeeping, I inherited the role of Family Hero. Complete with invisible cape, sparkling crown, and a crushing pile of emotional labor no one warned me about. And here's the kicker: I didn't even have it all together. I wasn't quiet. I wasn't tidy. I was loud, reactive, and sometimes an emotional tornado. But I was still the one everyone leaned on.

The fixer. The organizer. The "make it better" girl. And I've questioned it all. Did I claim that role because I needed control? Because I thought things would fall apart if I didn't hold it all together? Or was I just the only one willing to show the hell up when it mattered? Maybe that's why I looked like the strong one. Not because I was unshakable, but because I kept standing even when I was falling apart inside.

Either way, suddenly, I was the one people called when shit hit the fan. Not because I had magical powers or unlimited capacity, but because I made it *look* like I could handle anything.

Someone needed a mediator for a sibling fight? Me.

A buffer between Mom and her passive-aggressive spiral? Me again. A holiday plan, a ride to the airport, a last-minute casserole, a solution to someone else's emotional trainwreck? You guessed it, also me.

And don't get me wrong, I'm good at it. Like, very good.

I can organize a family gathering, talk someone off a ledge, and keep six relatives from murdering each other over mashed potatoes. But being good at something doesn't mean it's good for *you*.

By my late thirties, the cracks were starting to show. Not just stress, but soul-deep fatigue. A bone-tired burnout that no nap, no bubble bath, no "treat yourself" moment could fix. Because I wasn't just tired, I was depleted. I had spent years putting myself last to keep everyone else afloat, and the emotional overdraft notices were finally catching up.

The irony isn't lost on me. I was the one who showed up, held space, kept the peace, and carried emotional weight that didn't belong to me. Yet somehow, I'm the one who always got labeled selfish. Self-centered. As if choosing myself at any point in my life made me the villain.

There were moments, simple ones, where the weight hit me hard.

I'd say no to a family outing because I just didn't have it in me, and my sister would reply, *"Well, if you're not going, I'm not going."* And just like that, the responsibility of *everyone's day* landed squarely back on my shoulders. My options? Drag myself out with a fake smile and a silent scream or stay home and carry the guilt of "ruining it" for everyone else.

No matter what, I lost.

It wasn't always the big stuff, either. Sometimes it was just the *defaultness* of it all.

Being the one people expected to keep the peace, smooth it over, hold the line, fix the vibe. I accepted that role like it was my divine calling. Like keeping the family from imploding was *my* job.

Even when it drained me. Even when I was silently unraveling behind the scenes.

Eventually, I retired. No big announcement. No rage quit. I just...stopped. Stopped volunteering. Stopped offering first. Stopped absorbing everyone else's emotions like a human sponge with a savior complex.

And guess what? The world didn't end. People adjusted. *Or they didn't.*

Letting go of the cape didn't mean I stopped loving my family. It meant I finally started loving *myself*, too. It meant realizing that love isn't measured by how much pain you can hold. That loyalty doesn't mean abandoning yourself. That being strong? Sometimes it means letting people figure shit out on their own. Even if it's messy. Even if they're mad. Even if they call you selfish.

If you're reading this and feel like the designated glue holding everyone together, ask yourself this: *Who's holding you?*

If the answer is *no one*, maybe it's time to set the cape down. You've done enough. You don't have to save everyone to be worthy. You just have to save yourself.

And baby, that's the most heroic thing of all.

For Anyone Who's Always Been the "Strong One"

People get real comfortable leaning on you when they know you'll never say no. But let's be honest, do any of them ever stop to ask how much it's costing you?

That's not love. That's convenience.

And you? You deserve more than being someone's emotional life raft while they drift through their drama like you're the cruise director.

So go ahead, retire the cape. Let the calls go to voicemail.
Let the group chat figure itself out without your project-managing soul holding the whole operation together.

The world will keep spinning without your constant sacrifice.
The holidays will still happen. People will survive if they have to cook their own damn casserole.

Start holding space for *your* peace. Your dreams. Your healing.
Because when you finally start choosing yourself? That's not selfish. That's sacred.

And the day you stop performing for people who only love you for your usefulness?

That's the day you get your life back.

If your unconditional
love has conditions,
go ahead and
un-condition me
right out of that
group chat.

Chapter 5:
Family Forever? Bitch, Where?

Blood doesn't mean loyalty; sometimes it means war.

Growing up, I clung hard to the idea that family was everything. That no matter how bad it got, divorces, distance, dramatic Thanksgivings, you just showed up. You forgave. You moved on. You loved through it. That belief was gospel in my world. Unquestioned. Untouchable.

And then real life showed up, flipped the table, and said, "That's cute, babe, but here's how this *actually* works."

It started at a funeral. My uncle passed away, and just like that, my mom's family stopped speaking to his wife and kids. Poof. Gone. Like someone erased their names from the family tree with one bitter breath. A few years later, my aunt died and yep, you guessed it, same damn thing. No grief support, no circle of casseroles and comfort. Just more silence. More severed ties.

When another aunt was dying of cancer, you'd think people would come together. Rally. Be decent. But no. Instead, chaos broke out like wildfire. Whispers. Accusations. Emotional arson that tore our family in half. While she was still *alive*. While we should've been loving her through her final days, the only thing anyone passed around was blame.

The mess didn't end there. My sister had a small, intentional wedding. Quiet. Peaceful. Lovely. And because not everyone was invited, some relatives took it personally; like she'd burned down their house instead of just curating a guest list. The fallout? They didn't just cut her off. They cut *all* of us off. Like we were collateral damage in their personal offense parade.

And believe it or not, they didn't wait politely in the wings. These people were *actively* texting their outrage during the wedding. Not before. Not after. *During.* While vows were being exchanged and champagne was being poured, phones were lighting up with hateful messages - not just to the bride, but to the guests who had the audacity to attend. It wasn't disappointment. It was full-on emotional terrorism in real time. Like somehow their absence gave them moral superiority and front-row seats to sabotage.

Imagine for a minute being so offended you can't even let someone have one peaceful, joyful day without making it about *you*. That's not hurt feelings, that's narcissism in a group chat.

It's not just one side of the family, either. My dad hasn't spoken to two of his brothers in years. Over something that probably made sense in 1985 but sounds like bad sitcom drama now. He recently found out the full truth about something that happened decades ago. And still? He'd rather stew in resentment than reconcile. Because apparently, pride ages like a fine wine if you never open the damn bottle.

And then came the heartbreak I didn't see coming. My sister and her oldest daughter just…left. No conversation. No final words. Just silence. A slow fade-out wrapped in the ever-convenient phrase, "This is my boundary." And listen, I *believe* in boundaries. Healthy ones. Honest ones. But when silence is used as a weapon instead of a healing tool, it doesn't feel like growth. It feels like punishment.

Social media is a double-edged sword. I love a good quote carousel with floral backgrounds and dreamy fonts. Hell, I've reposted my fair share. But what really grinds my gears is when a full-blown narcissist scrolls past one of those "protect your peace" or "boundaries are healthy" posts and somehow decides *they're* the enlightened one. Like…no, Karen, walking away from your family without a word and calling it a boundary isn't growth; it's avoidance dressed up in Canva fonts.

Boundaries require communication. They require honesty, discomfort, and sometimes repair. Not a disappearing act and a vague post about "choosing yourself." Let's not confuse emotional maturity with emotional manipulation just because the lighting was good on your quote graphic.

The hardest part? I still want to believe in the fairytale version of family. The one where grief brings people together. Where weddings are holy. Where love holds tighter than petty drama. But here's what I know: *family isn't blood, it's behavior.* It's the people who show up, not just the ones who share your last name.

Some families fracture quietly. Others explode. Mine? We did both. But instead of keeping the score, I've started keeping boundaries.

Because I'd rather have peace than forced tradition.

I'd rather have honesty than obligation.

If that means building my own version of family from scratch?

So be it.

For Anyone Who Had to Grieve the Living to Save Themselves

The truth is that family can break your heart deeper than anyone else. They're supposed to be your safe place. Your constants. But sometimes they're your first betrayal. Your longest lesson. And that's okay to admit. You're allowed to grieve the people who are still alive. You're allowed to choose yourself, even when it means choosing distance.

You don't have to keep performing for people who stopped clapping. You can stop begging to be understood. You can stop holding on to the version of family you *wish* you had and start making space for the one you're building now; the one that chooses you, every time.

Grief doesn't always come dressed in black and show up at funerals. Sometimes it looks like silence after a holiday. Sometimes it's the ache of being in the same room with people who feel like strangers. And sometimes, it's realizing that being related by blood doesn't mean you're bonded by love.

That kind of grief is sneaky. It lingers. And it hurts like hell because there's no closure; just the slow, painful acceptance that they may never become who you needed them to be.

Here's what you *can* do: stop watering dead plants. Stop sacrificing your sanity for people who never learned how to love you properly. Build your own version of family with the people who see you, hear you, and hold you without conditions. It won't look like the picture you grew up imagining, but it'll be real. And safe. And yours.

Turns out, your boundary was just you vanishing like a magician with unresolved trauma.

Chapter 6:

Wait…You Hate Me?

AKA: The Grief of Loving Someone Who Disappeared Without Dying

There's heartbreak, and then there's the gut-punch that comes when your own sister, your closest person, just…goes silent. You could have never imagined your last call would be *the last* call. One day, it was conversations, laughter, shared secrets. The next, it was static. Emptiness. An invisible line drawn in the sand, and somehow, I'd already crossed it.

She knew everything. Every deep, dark detail. She was the one I went to when the world felt like it was eating me alive. She was my safe place before I even understood what that meant. Her oldest daughter? Felt like mine. Maybe that was the problem. Maybe I loved her daughter too hard. Got too close. Did too much. Maybe I blurred the lines of sister and second mom. I don't know. I've had years to guess. That doesn't mean I've gotten any closer to an answer.

I went trick-or-treating with her two younger children for most of their childhoods. Me, an adult with no kids of my own, dressed up, holding candy buckets, laughing like I belonged there. And in those moments, I thought I did. I was in their photos, their memories, their day-to-day lives. I wasn't a guest, I was part of the fabric.

I supported my oldest niece through her hardest moments. Helped her raise her child while she was trying to piece her life back together. I gave everything I had to give, and I never kept score. That's the thing about love; you give it without expecting a receipt.

I showed up. Over and over and over again. I didn't just love them; I committed to them. With my time, my heart, my energy. I rearranged my life to make space for theirs. Because that's what family does. At least, that's what I believed. That's what I *still* want to believe, even now.

And then, one day, it was just over

The break didn't start with my sister, at least not directly. It started with my niece. One day, without warning, there were suddenly "boundaries" in place. Not shared with me in conversation, not offered with care or clarity, but hurled at my mother in sharp, angry tones. I tried to understand. I tried to honor her feelings, even when they didn't make sense to me. I told my mom it was okay, that we should just give her time, that she was working through something.

But when you're deeply woven into someone's daily life for so many years, through holidays, heartbreaks, and every ordinary Tuesday, walking away isn't easy or clean. The emotional ties were real, and messy, and I think somewhere in all that mess, we all got overwhelmed. Emotions ran high. And eventually, everything broke.

What I never imagined would happen is that my sister would disappear with her. I was blocked. Texts, calls, every social media platform. Like I was a threat. Like I was dangerous. Like my name had suddenly become a bad word.

Every birthday, every holiday, I still reached out. For five years. I kept sending love into a void that never echoed back. At first, I gave them space. For months, I told myself they just needed time. That the silence wasn't permanent, just a pause. I honored their boundary; even when it didn't come with context, even when it hurt.

Those months turned into years. And still, nothing. No reply. No explanation. Just a growing ache where connection used to be. Hope is a stubborn thing. It'll keep whispering maybe this time even when the answer's been "no" for years.

But one day, after leaving three tearful, begging voicemails, I received a message in Facebook messenger:

"Sis, you know I have always and will always love you dearly. I don't really know anything else to say but that."

That was it. No explanation. No apology. Just a soft reminder that I was still loved…but apparently not enough to be let back in. Not enough to earn a conversation. Not enough to matter in the way I had once mattered.

Grieving someone who's still alive is a special kind of hell. Especially when that someone used to be your everything. They still post. They still laugh. They still exist in the same world as you, but not *with* you. It's like watching a life you once belonged to continue without your chapter in it.

I don't know fully what happened. I may never know. And that's its own kind of grief, the grief of ambiguity. Of unfinished stories and unanswered questions. Of turning something over in your mind until it loses all shape and meaning. Closure never came. Maybe it never will.

Here's what I've learned: Love without access is a ghost. And I'm tired of being haunted.

Sometimes the deepest pain doesn't come from betrayal.

It comes from the silence that follows it.

From not knowing what you did wrong.

From never getting the chance to make it right.

From watching someone shut the door without giving you a chance to knock.

I've learned that love doesn't always come with logic. And closure? It's a luxury, not a guarantee. But peace? That's mine to claim. Even if it comes without a goodbye. Even if I have to build it from scraps. Even if I have to stop asking "why" and start saying "enough."

Because healing doesn't wait for explanations. It begins the moment you stop begging for one.

Even still, if my absence was the price for them to finally have the relationship they'd spent years fighting for but never fully held, I would pay it. Gladly. I would walk away, quietly, if it meant my niece could feel the kind of love every daughter deserves from her mother.

For Anyone Still Waiting for an Explanation That May Never Come

Losing someone without losing them to death is its own category of heartbreak. And when the silence stays longer than the bond ever did, it carves a hollow place inside you. But you are not broken, you're just holding space for something that never got finished.

You don't need their closure to build your peace. You don't need their permission to heal. If they can't meet you with clarity, meet *yourself* with compassion. You're allowed to grieve. You're allowed to move on. And you're allowed to stop answering a door that's been locked from the other side.

Maybe one day they'll reach out. Maybe they won't. But either way, you don't have to keep putting your life on pause, waiting for someone else to explain why they left you standing in the wreckage.

You don't owe your healing to a conversation that may never happen. That empty seat at your emotional table? Let it stay empty. You don't need to keep setting a place for someone who chose to walk away.

Closure isn't a gift they give you; it's a boundary you build for yourself. It's choosing to stop replaying the past like it'll suddenly make sense if you just hurt long enough. It's deciding that your peace matters more than the mystery. You can write your own ending, even if theirs never shows up. That's not giving up. That's growing up.

If your version of events skips over
your own behavior...tell it to your
diary, not your therapist.

Chapter 7:
Tell Your Therapist the Whole Story, Babe

Especially the parts where you weren't the victim.

There's a special kind of betrayal that comes from someone getting close enough to know your wounds, then slicing them open on purpose. They don't just hurt you, they *study* you. Learn your soft spots. Memorize your scars. Then, with precision, they turn all of it against you. It's calculated. Surgical. And it leaves you bleeding in ways that no one else can see.

They twist the most broken, whispered parts of you into weapons. The things you told them in confidence, in weakness, in late-night survival mode? The secrets you shared because you thought you were safe? Those become ammo. The pain you were brave enough to speak out loud is suddenly thrown back at you like evidence in a trial you didn't know you were part of.

I've had more than one narcissistic ex (so if you're reading this and thinking, "Wait, which one?" ...same). These were men who knew I struggled with memory. Who knew I'd trained myself to forget pain as a survival tactic. Who watched me fumble for clarity in the middle of emotional fog and nodded like they understood. Like they cared. They nodded while making mental notes, not for empathy, but for *strategy*.

And what did they do with that knowledge?

They turned it into a script. *Their* script. A version of reality where I was always wrong. Always irrational. Always "too much." And they were always the calm, logical ones just trying to deal with my "crazy."

It always started small. A disagreement. A detail I remembered with perfect clarity. Not a blurry moment. Not a dream. *The truth*. But suddenly, I was being told, "That's not how it happened." Or worse, "That never happened at all."

"You're being dramatic."
"You're remembering it wrong."
"You're always so sensitive."

And just like that, I was spiraling. Shaking. Replaying conversations in my head. Digging through texts, rereading messages, trying to prove something to *myself* because no one else seemed to care if I was right. And when someone you love tells you enough times that your memory is broken, your trust in yourself starts to break with it.

Gaslighting isn't just lying, it's psychological warfare. It's a slow, strategic erasure of your inner voice. It's someone handing you a version of your own life that *almost* feels right, but is just twisted enough to leave you dizzy and doubting everything you thought you knew. And when someone's already cracked open your soul and bookmarked your insecurities? That doubt multiplies. Fast. Loud. All-consuming.

This wasn't just about control. It was about keeping me small. Because if I couldn't trust my memory, I had to trust theirs. If I couldn't prove the truth, I had to *accept* theirs. And that? That's a quiet kind of hell. One that doesn't leave bruises but breaks you just the same. A hell where you start apologizing for things you didn't do, reacting to things that never happened, questioning feelings that were completely valid.

They say knowledge is power, but in the wrong hands, your truth becomes a trap. They don't want to destroy you in one blow; they want you to unravel yourself. Piece by piece. Doubt by doubt. Until you don't even recognize who you were before them.

Healing meant learning how to trust myself again. To stop fact-checking my memories like I was unreliable by default. To stop handing over my reality to someone who treated it like a draft they had full editorial rights over. To believe in my own memory, even when someone tried to erase it. To know, deeply and without apology, that anyone who uses your trauma as leverage was never safe to begin with.

These days? I'm the author of my story. And if anyone tries to edit it without permission? They can kindly get the hell out of the narrative.

No rewrites. No revisions. No second chances. Just the truth, unfiltered and fully mine.

For Anyone Gaslit Into Questioning Their Own Reality

If someone ever made you doubt your memory, your sanity, your truth, hear this: *You were not crazy.* You were being conditioned. Manipulated. Gaslit. The fact that you're here, reading this, reclaiming your story? That's strength.

Your memory is valid. Your feelings are real. You don't need their permission to believe yourself. Trust your gut. Take up space. And never again hand your truth to someone who doesn't know how to hold it gently.

Gaslighting doesn't always show up as screaming and slamming doors. Sometimes it's a soft smile paired with "you're too sensitive," or a casual rewrite of events that leaves you questioning your grip on reality.

That's the insidious part; it trains you to doubt yourself so deeply that even your instincts feel like a liability. But guess what? The fog is lifting now. And clarity looks damn good on you.

You're no longer the person who swallows discomfort just to keep the peace. You're no longer afraid to say, "That definitely happened," even if they pretend it didn't.

Let them squirm under the weight of your truth. It's not your job to make it more comfortable for them. It's your job to honor it. You don't have to be polite about your healing. You just have to be honest.

And relentless.

Every day someone wakes up and
chooses delusion over decency.

Chapter 8:
The Audacity Chronicles

Where do people find the nerve? Seriously. Is there a clearance rack?

Please hold while I search for where people get the nerve.

Okay, I'm back.

Trigger warning: this chapter gets real. Because life did.

Let's talk about audacity: that bold, brazen confidence people somehow summon to say or do the most shocking, violating, WTF-level things. From flippant comments to full-on trauma, I've seen it all. Lived it. There's a spectrum, and unfortunately, I've been hit with every shade of it.

The kind that leaves you speechless in the moment, then furious hours later when the right words finally show up. But by then, it's too late and they've already moved on like nothing happened.

It starts small, sometimes. A male cousin crosses a line. An inappropriate moment brushed off by adults with, "Boys will be boys," or "They're just figuring *things* out."

Excuse me? Figuring out what, exactly? And why is it always at *our* expense? Why is our discomfort the price of their learning curve?

I didn't have the words back then, but I knew it felt wrong. I knew that frozen feeling, that internal shutdown, that desperate wish to just disappear. What I didn't have was the audacity to speak up. Because I'd already learned that when I did, the adults would twist themselves into pretzels to explain it away. They were Olympic-level mental gymnasts when it came to protecting *them*. But not me.

So, the next time it happened? When a man, married into my family, crept into the room while I was sleeping and put his hands where they absolutely did not belong?

I stayed quiet. I protected *him*. Because that's what we were taught: how to carry their secrets and shoulder their shame like it was ours. How to shrink. How to rationalize. How to survive. Because speaking up wasn't just scary, it was punished. You became "dramatic." "Confused." "Too sensitive." So we buried it. Deep. And let the silence rot our insides.

And it doesn't stop in childhood.

Grown-up me? She's had a front-row seat to the same damn pattern. Exes who couldn't take "no" for an answer. That slow, insistent pressure. That relentless wearing down of boundaries like waves on a rock. That push until you give in, not out of desire, but out of sheer exhaustion. Just make it stop. Just get it over with.

And then comes the guilt. The numbness. The shame. The mental tug-of-war between "Was that assault?" and "Well, I didn't fight harder, so maybe it wasn't."

Let me stop you right there and let me be loud and clear:

Your body is yours. Husband, boyfriend, partner - none of them are entitled to it.

Consent is not a one-time vow you give at the altar. It's not baked into a relationship title. It's a "yes" or "no" every single time. Period. And anything less than *freely given, enthusiastic consent* is not okay.

Sometimes I look around at what people do and say and genuinely wonder if I missed some sort of bulk discount on audacity.

Like… could you not? Could you *just not?*

Like the coworker who makes comments about your outfit with a smirk. Like the relative who "jokes" about your body like it's theirs to critique. Like the man who gets offended when you dare to have boundaries. Where do they get the confidence? Did it ship free with their entitlement? Was it buy one, get gaslighting free?

But their audacity is not my burden. Their shame is not mine to carry. What happened to me wasn't my fault, but healing *is* my responsibility. And healing looks like rage. Like softness. Like truth. Like boundaries. It looks like finally, *finally*, saying: You don't get to rewrite what happened. You don't get to guilt me into silence. You don't get to live freely while I drown in the aftermath.

I do. I get to rise. I get to speak. And I get to burn every unspoken rule that ever asked me to stay small just so someone else could feel big.

For Anyone Still Carrying What Wasn't Theirs to Carry

If you've been touched, talked to, pressured, or pushed in ways that made your skin crawl, whether it was brushed off or buried, you are not alone. You never were. We grow up being told to be polite. To protect the family name. To stay quiet so we don't "make it worse." But silence doesn't protect *us*. It protects *them*.

Let's stop swallowing our pain to make other people comfortable.

Let's reclaim what was always ours: our voice, our bodies, our boundaries.

Let their shame be *theirs* to carry.

And that audacity? Let's return it to sender, no refund.

You were never too sensitive. You were never overreacting. You were surviving in a world that taught you to question yourself instead of confronting the people who hurt you. That's not your burden to carry anymore.

The guilt? The shame? The responsibility for what someone else did? Drop it. Set it down like the dead weight it is. You don't owe your silence to anyone who made you feel unsafe.

Healing doesn't need to look pretty. It can be messy, loud, angry, and real. You get to rewrite the rules. You get to scream when you were told to whisper. You get to say what happened, and not need a damn thing from the people who looked away. What was done to you doesn't define you, but how you rise from it absolutely does.

And baby, you're rising loud, unbothered, and unbreakable.

Our family had thorns,
loose branches, and
a court ordered
visitation schedule.

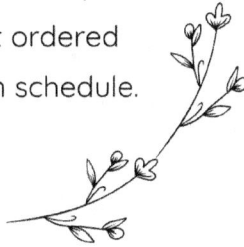

Chapter 9:

Blended, Bruised, and Boundaries

Because "family" isn't an excuse for emotional malnourishment.

Blending families sounds cute on paper.

More siblings! More birthdays! Matching PJs for Christmas!

But let me tell you that what it actually looks like is *complicated as hell*, especially when the adults in charge never quite figure out how to balance their old lives with their shiny new ones.

I remember exactly how it started. My sister and our soon-to-be stepsisters introduced our parents. Yep, this entire Brady Bunch chaos was technically our fault. We were just kids, hanging out every other weekend down the street from each other near my dad's house. It felt like a fun little crossover episode. Until it didn't.

The idea of gaining two more sisters our age? At first, it was exciting. Something bright in a house that often felt cold and divided. But the older we got, the more the cracks showed…*especially* the gaping one that formed from watching our dad raise a whole new family while barely showing up for his own.

As we got older, our stepmom made it crystal clear that our existence was an inconvenience. Every time my dad had to come over to fix something or show up for anything remotely resembling parenting, she'd roll her eyes and ask, "Where's your mom?" as if us needing our father was somehow our mother's failure.

She constantly complained that they were broke because of all the child support he was supposedly paying, which was wild, considering we barely ever saw a dime and he was barely around.

She hated that we'd call the house and ask for him directly, skipping pleasantries, skipping her. But what did she expect? He was a ghost at best, and when he did materialize, it wasn't because of her.

She blamed us for the tension, but we were just kids trying to reach a dad who didn't show up unless it was convenient. Another family, maybe? That cat's still in the bag…but trust me, it's clawing to get out.

Let me paint a picture.

I was TWENTY-SEVEN when my parents had a court date…to deal with unpaid child support. You may be asking yourself why he was still paying child support nine years after he was obligated by law to do so? Because that money my stepmom claimed was going to my mom every week didn't actually make it to my mom…shocking, I know.

The week before that hearing, while my maternal grandmother was literally dying in the hospital, my father came and sat down next to me in the waiting room. You may be thinking he was there to support his children, his ex-wife and her family, as he was once part of this family.

Nope. His first and only words were:

"If you don't get your mom to drop the payments next week in court, I'll never speak to any of you again."

Let that *marinate.*

I was grieving, exhausted, and sitting with my family near my dying grandmother. And somehow, *still* expected to be the family's emotional glue. I got up. I left the room. And I sobbed down the hallway, in the elevator and all the way outside. A *stranger* stopped and asked me if I was okay. My own father? Walked right past me. No words. No eye contact.

In court? My mom did what he wanted. She dropped the payments.

And still…he stopped talking to us.

I was so desperate to make it make sense that I even wrote my stepmom a letter (yes, an *actual* letter…this was pre-text era, give me a break). I needed answers. I needed to understand how she could be okay standing next to a man who had so casually disowned his daughters like we were seasonal acquaintances he outgrew. Especially since she'd spent years critiquing the kind of care my mom gave us. I figured, surely, she'd have some thoughts on her husband cutting us off entirely.

Spoiler alert: she did. Just not the thoughts I thought a person in this circumstance would have.

The venom in that letter? Hall. Of. Fame. Level.

She said my sisters and I were "full of [insert maiden name here] blood" and that she'd never understand how people could be so hateful.

Which is *wild*, because…ma'am, you married into said family and this so called hateful blood is raising *your* daughters.

Years passed. We went no contact. And then one day, she reached out. Lovingly, even. Told me my grandfather had died. Said she was sorry for everything. Said it was time to move forward, be a family again. And I believed her. We all did. We came back. We tried.

My dad? Never acknowledged anything. No ownership. No apology. Just strolled back into our lives like nothing ever happened. Like emotional abandonment has an expiration date.

These days, we don't speak. I haven't talked to him in years. And every day in my healing journey, I remind myself that you don't have to stay where you're not fed. Even if it's "family." *Especially* if it's family.

Now here's the twist:

My sister has flipped the script. Since disowning us, she's become thick as thieves with him, and his stepdaughters. The same niece who used to say she wouldn't invite her grandfather anywhere if his wife was coming? Her wish has finally come true. My stepmom has passed, and now she's able to have him front and center in her life.

My sister? Followed his blueprint. Walked away from the people who loved her most and aligned herself with the one who taught us how to disappear. It wasn't healing and boundaries. It was legacy.

And me? I'm just watching, again, from the outside of a family that I was always expected to *fix*, but never allowed to *feel safe* in.

Blending families isn't about mixing people. It's about managing expectations, emotions, and the ghosts of unhealed wounds. And when those wounds are ignored, they don't fade, they get inherited.

Being the glue in a family sounds noble until you realize you're the one always getting stuck. These days, I don't blend. I build. And I only sit at tables where I'm not the only one bringing peace.

For Anyone Who's Been the Glue, the Ghost, or the Scapegoat

You don't owe anyone access to you just because they share your blood. You're allowed to walk away from what hurts, even if it wears the title "family." You don't have to be the fixer, the forgiver, or the emotional punching bag. You are not responsible for healing wounds you didn't create. Build your own peace. Create your own family. Choose people who choose *you*. Again and again *without conditions*.

If they only love you when you're convenient, when you're quiet, helpful, or carrying the blame, then that's not love. That's control dressed up in tradition. And you're not here to be the family mascot, the scapegoat for their dysfunction, or the ghost who disappears to keep the peace. You get to exist fully. Loudly. Authentically. Without shrinking to fit inside the boxes they built for their own comfort.

You don't need a big dramatic exit. Sometimes the most radical thing you can do is simply stop showing up for people who never showed up for you.

Let them call it selfish. Let them spin their stories.

You've got better things to do. Like healing, thriving, and surrounding yourself with people who don't just *tolerate* you, but celebrate the hell out of you.

That's the real definition of family.

She got the husband,
I got the peace.
Honestly? I won.

Chapter 10:

He Got a New Wife. I Got My Sanity Back.

Guess who's thriving.

I wasn't that little girl planning her dream wedding. No Pinterest board of centerpieces. No rehearsed vows in the mirror. If you'd asked eight-year-old me about marriage, I probably would've said, *"Hard pass."*

So why did I sprint into one? Two words: daddy issues.

If a man looked semi-responsible and had a pulse, I was probably ready to walk down the aisle. Not because I believed in happily-ever-after, but because I believed maybe, *just maybe*, love could fix the cracks that started way before he ever showed up.

When I met my now ex-husband, my then-boyfriend had just moved out of state. Emotionally? I was not okay. But I wore my finest mask: Life-of-the-party mode. Always smiling. Always fine. Always the "you good?" friend.

The truth? We had been together for years. He was my person. My plan. And then one day, just like that, he packed up and left for a job in another state. No cheating, no blow-up, just ambition, timing, and suddenly I was here…without him.

We tried the long-distance thing. The calls, the visits, the forced normalcy. But when you're in your early twenties and all your friends are going out every night, it's really easy to fall off track. To chase a little attention. To end up in beds that weren't part of the original plan. Oops.

It wasn't malicious, it was lonely. And messy. And human. And somewhere in that whirlwind, I met someone new. A distraction that turned into a detour that became a decade-long lesson.

I was deep in my party girl era, where tequila fixed everything and the dance floor doubled as therapy. We met at a bar (because of course we did). I was out living my best chaotic life, and he was standing off to the side…barking at me.

Yes. *Barking.*

Like a damn dog in cargo shorts.

And instead of running? My intoxicated brain said, *"Yes, this is how love starts."*

By the end of the night, he was in my car with all my friends and just like that, we were a thing.

You know that saying, "You can't turn a hoe into a househusband"? That *is* how it goes, right? Well, turns out, they were absolutely right. I went into it like I was on some kind of DIY boyfriend makeover show. Thought I'd be the one to change him. Smooth out the chaos, polish the edges, earn my gold star for turning a mess into marriage material.

Spoiler alert: that didn't happen.

What *did* happen was years of gut feelings I couldn't explain. Trust with him was always…fragile. Like glass on a ledge. And for the longest time, I couldn't figure out why, because I *wanted* to believe him. I convinced myself I was just overthinking, being insecure, making things up in my head.

Then we split. And guess who still kept calling, texting, checking in like we were still a thing…all while he was already knee-deep in a new relationship?

That's when it clicked: I wasn't crazy. I wasn't insecure. I was married to someone who simply wasn't honest. With me, with her, probably not even with himself.

If his current wife thinks she's the exception? That she's the one who "fixed" him? Girl, good luck. I guarantee that he's not the man you think he is. I've got the receipts, and the emotional whiplash, to prove it.

Here's the thing about being in the First Wives Club. It's a masterclass in trial and error.

You don't just grow together. You grow *up* together. You're broke, overwhelmed, emotionally undercooked, and navigating each other's baggage like you're playing a relationship game show with no instructions and no prize money.

I got the "full frontal lobe not yet developed" starter-pack:

- Bonus baby mama baggage
- In-laws divorcing the second we said "I do"
- His depression, with a side of suicidal threats like it was my emotional job to fix it
- And adulting like I was auditioning for a burnout documentary

We had no business being married. We were two broken people trying to play house. And yet, we kept trying. For a while? We were best friends in the realest way. Inside jokes. Fast food in bed.

Trauma bonding strong enough to *almost* believe it was forever.

But being best friends doesn't mean you're meant to be. We needed healing, not a honeymoon. Eventually, the cracks we ignored turned into canyons we couldn't cross.

Somewhere in the middle of the unraveling, he started making new "friends". Ones outside our circle, far removed from the people who had seen us through the real shit.

It started when a girl at the gym said, *"You'd get along with my husband."* Cute. Next thing I know, he's ghosting his longtime business partner, dodging accountability, and chasing a lifestyle he once scoffed at but suddenly decided would "fix" him.

He didn't just leave the relationship, he ran toward a version of himself he thought would finally be enough. New crew. New image. New narrative. Same old avoidance.

While he sprinted into the sunset with people he once envied, convinced they'd give him the validation he'd been starving for, I stayed behind. With the mess, the silence, and eventually...the peace.

Being the *first* wife means you got the version of him still under construction; blueprints drawn in trauma, and tools made of red flags. It doesn't mean you failed. It means you showed up. You gave love. You probably stayed longer than you should have.

You weren't stupid. You were *hopeful.* You were *brave.*

And now? Now you're smarter. Softer in the right places and sharper in the ones that matter.

You don't need to apologize for loving fully. You just need to promise yourself that you will never settle for almost again.

For the First Wives, the Failed Loves, and the Finally Healed

Being the "first" anything doesn't make you a failure. It makes you the blueprint. You learned the hard way, the heartbreaking way, the hilarious way. You learned what love is *not*, and now you get to build the version of life that finally makes sense.

You were never "too much", you were just with someone not equipped to meet you there. Wear your experience like armor, not shame. Your next chapter? It's written in self-worth, peace, and joy that doesn't come with conditions.

Let them whisper about how it ended. Let them call it a phase, a failure, a fallout. You know what it really was? A fucking awakening. You didn't just survive heartbreak; you outgrew a life that was too small for you. You walked through the fire and came out with clarity, boundaries, and one hell of a sense of humor. That's not failure. That's freedom in a pair of cute sneakers.

You're not bitter, you're better. Better at spotting red flags. Better at protecting your peace. Better at loving yourself so fiercely that anything less feels laughable.

Here's to the firsts, the lessons, and the letdowns that shaped you. They didn't break you; they built you. And now? You get to write the rest of your story like the main character you've always been.

I wasn't thinking. I was trauma-bonding and romanticizing red flags like they were fireworks.

Chapter 11:
Girl, What Were You Thinking?

Every woman has that *story. This one is mine.*

Every woman has at least one story that makes her cringe so hard she wants to jump in a time machine and slap herself.

This is mine.

It started with a reconnection; comfort disguised as closure.

I found myself with someone who had once been my ex's best friend. He'd been part of my life story once before, and now (after the sudden loss of my ex, the grief, and the chaos that followed) there was history. Familiarity. That dangerous "he understands me" feeling.

As far as I knew, he wasn't in a relationship. *Because that is what he said.* He told me he lived with his brother, about 30 minutes away. Gave no reason not to trust him. Claimed to be a Godly man, full of growth and redemption and all the right buzzwords that make you think, "Hmm… maybe he's changed."

Spoiler: he hadn't.

Everything I once knew about him, the reality, the history, the instinct I should've trusted, suddenly left my brain like someone had hit Ctrl+Alt+Del on my common sense. I wanted to believe the version he was selling: reformed, steady, rooted in faith. But the receipts didn't match the story.

There were red flags. Loud ones. Like, DEFCON 1 waving in my face. He didn't have a relationship with his daughter; blamed her mom and stepdad for "turning her against him." His relationship with his sons? Strained, at best; but that was *their* fault, too. And yet, every five minutes he was telling me how *deeply* he valued family. Sir, where?

Add in the fact that he used to be a ladies' man (and had no shame about it), I probably should've known he wasn't going to suddenly become monogamy's poster child. My ex even kept us apart for most of our relationship. Probably because he knew if his best friend so much as caught me at a vulnerable moment, he'd shoot his shot like we were in a Hallmark movie with a toxic twist.

Cut to a year after we reconnected.

I find out this man, that I've been emotionally and physically wrapped up in, has been in a full-blown, *years-long* relationship with someone else. Not only were they still together...they lived together.

So, yes. I was the *other woman*. And had absolutely *no idea*.

Did he confess? Admit anything? Show even a sliver of remorse? Of course not! That would require accountability. He was fully committed to his lie. Which is about the only thing he will commit to.

What did I do? What any woman with a side of righteous fury does: I reached out to her. The other woman. The *actual* girlfriend. And her response? Not even close to what I expected.

"That sounds like an issue you need to discuss with him. Leave me out of it."

Um...*excuse me?* I wasn't asking for your tax records. I asked if y'all were still together. A simple "yes" or "no" would've sufficed.

Apparently, she already knew. Not just about me but also about *others*. Plural.

And yet for the next FOUR YEARS (yes, full caps are earned) I stayed in contact with him.

I wasn't in a healthy headspace. I convinced myself I needed the familiarity, the comfort, the "maybe this time will be different" fairytale I'd rewritten in my head a hundred times. What I *really* needed was therapy and a block button.

The gaslighting? Guinness World Record-worthy.

I lost count of how many other women came out of the woodwork. Different names, same script. Turns out, I wasn't special. I was just part of a casting call he kept rerunning. Each woman believed the same recycled fairytale I did: that she was the one he'd finally get it right for. Meanwhile, he was out here freelancing heartbreak like it paid commission.

His stories started unraveling mid-sentence. Timelines didn't add up. Details shifted. Alibis crumbled. At one point, I had more receipts than Target on Black Friday. It wasn't just lies; it was a whole damn anthology. And still, somehow, he had the audacity to act like *I* was the crazy one.

Eventually, we drifted apart. Or maybe I just finally floated up from the toxic sludge I'd been willingly wading in. We only talk occasionally now. The last time? After he got engaged. To, *you guessed it*, the original girlfriend I reached out to years ago.

You can't make this stuff up.

I sent a half-hearted "I guess I should say congrats," and he hit me back with multiple too long messages, but here's the gist:

"I haven't decided if I'm going through with it."
"We reconnected when her mom got sick, and it just happened."
"She still has things to work on."
"Can I just see you in person and talk about everything?"

Oh yes. Totally sounds like a changed man. Bless her heart. Honestly.

I stayed because I craved *comfort*, not chaos. But comfort from a liar isn't love, it's self-abandonment. I ignored the red flags. Believed the PR version.

When someone shows you their patterns, believe them. Even if they're hiding behind scripture and cologne.

And yes...*of course* I still have the receipts.

For Anyone Who Stayed Too Long for All the Wrong Reasons

You're not stupid for wanting to believe the best in someone. You're not weak for wanting love to be real. But here's the truth: love that costs you your dignity isn't love; it's a trap.

The lesson isn't just to leave when it's bad. It's to *stop returning* when someone shows you they have no intention of healing. You are not a rehab center. You're a whole damn person. Choose yourself, every single time.

You can keep hoping, helping, hurting, thinking *this time* might be different. But love doesn't spark change. Begging won't build growth. And setting yourself on fire for lukewarm love? Dumb.

If you stayed too long, forgive yourself. That wasn't weakness, it was hope. Now? Now it's time to hope for something *better*. Something peaceful. Something safe. Something that doesn't require you to abandon yourself to keep it.

Let them figure out their own healing. You've got a life to reclaim, and it starts the second you stop settling for scraps and start demanding the whole damn table.

You're not a detour.
You're the destination.

Chapter 12:
The Side Dish is Never the Main Course

If he lies to her, he'll lie to you.

As you can see from the previous chapter, I somehow landed squarely in the "other woman" category. *Again.* Not proudly. Not loudly. But definitely, unfortunately, yes, it happened.

Now, I'd love to tell you it was a one-time thing. That it was just a blip in my early twenties brought on by vodka, low self-worth, and abandonment issues that hadn't yet earned their therapy badges. But, no. The universe threw that test my way more than once. And let's be real, sometimes I went looking for it. Daddy issues are not a damn myth.

When women end up in these situations, we become Olympic-level gymnasts; flipping through excuses and contorting ourselves into delusion. "He's separated." "He's only there for the kids." "They don't even sleep in the same bed." "They're basically roommates."

Oh honey, I've said it, I've believed it, I've cried over it, and I've *defended* it like a lawyer trying to win a case they'll never possibly win.

Let me say this plain and LOUD: if he has to *sneak*, *lie*, or *disappear* to see you, then you are not in a relationship. You are in a poorly written subplot of a man's cowardice.

And yet, we do it. All the time. So many women I've met, strong, smart, gorgeous, magnetic women, have found themselves on the other side of the love triangle. It doesn't come with an official name badge. No one's out here proudly sporting "Mistress #2" in rhinestones. But it creeps in quietly, disguised as connection and chemistry and "it's complicated." Before you know it, you're parked outside his house waiting for a window light to turn off like a goddamn spy.

And you think, "Well, I'm different. I *get* him." Baby girl, you don't. You're just the one getting lied to *slightly* less.

When a man lies to his wife, the mother of his children, the person he vowed to love and protect, what in God's name makes us think he'll suddenly be honest with us? That somehow we've unlocked a version of him that's truthful, pure, and only misguided because *she* doesn't understand him? Please.

It took me a long, brutal, necessary journey to realize I didn't want to be anyone's secret anymore. That I don't have to earn love by accepting scraps. That hiding in the shadows of someone else's relationship doesn't make me desired, it makes me *disposable*.

The thing about being the other woman is that you're often treated like you should be flattered to even *be* an option. That somehow, you're special because he chose *you* to cheat with. Let me tell you. Being an option is not a compliment. It's a demotion.

I've learned that love isn't meant to be hidden behind excuses, ducked behind corners, or whispered through burner phones. Love stands tall. Love shows up. Love picks you. Publicly, consistently, and without condition.

To every woman reading this who's ever found herself in the passenger seat of a car she shouldn't be in, or wearing perfume that smells like guilt, I want you to hear this clearly: You deserve more. You deserve honesty. You deserve someone who claims you out loud and doesn't delete your texts. You deserve to be Plan A, not the *oops* after a night of regret.

This chapter isn't about shame, it's about *freedom*. The freedom that comes with no longer accepting relationships that dim your light. The freedom that says, "I will not compete with a woman who doesn't even know we're in a race."

I forgive that other version of me. I understand her now. She was craving love in the only language she knew at the time: attention. But

I've since learned a new language. One that sounds like peace, respect, and someone who doesn't flinch when my name shows up on their phone.

For Anyone Who's Ever Confused Drama for Devotion

You were never hard to love; you just kept auditioning for roles in someone else's script.

If you've ever been the other woman, or almost the other woman, or flirted with the idea of being the other woman because it felt safer than being rejected by someone single, this is your moment of clarity. It's not about shame. It's about *elevation*.

You don't need to be loved in secret. You don't need to shrink to fit into the cracks of someone else's broken promises. Walk away. Delete the number. Block the access. And repeat after me: I am not a backup plan. I am the whole damn future.

Being the other woman isn't just about him, it's also about what you believed about yourself at the time. Maybe you thought that kind of love was the best you could get. That a little was better than nothing. That you were strong enough to handle it.

But survival isn't the same as thriving. Real love won't make you feel like a secret. It won't ask you to question your worth. And it damn sure won't ask you to be quiet about who you are and how you feel. Your presence should never be something someone has to hide.

This is your reminder that you don't have to settle for halfway. You don't have to settle for "when the time is right" or "once things calm down." You are worthy of someone who shows up fully, not just when it's convenient. Someone who holds your hand in public, not just your thigh in private.

Here's your permission slip to demand more, expect better, and never again entertain anyone who treats you like a detour.

I don't have kids. But I
have snacks, opinions,
and a lot more sleep.

Chapter 13:

Not a Mom. But Still a Whole Damn Person.

I didn't get the baby. I got peace, clarity, and a front-row seat to my own freedom.

Let's talk about the kind of heartbreak that doesn't get a soundtrack. No slammed doors. No final goodbye. Just quiet little hopes that slowly disappear while you keep pretending that you're fine.

I was married, doing all the "next step" things. Ring? Check. House? Check. Next up? A baby. I thought I was ready. We tried. For over a year.

Ovulation apps, fertility trackers, green juice, acupuncture, and every woo-woo ritual you can imagine. I did it all. I peed on more sticks than I care to admit. Most of the time, my bathroom looked like a pregnancy test crime scene.

We finally saw a fertility specialist, and that's when the overwhelm hit me like a hormonal freight train. I didn't want to do it. The injections. The ultrasounds. The calendar of chaos. I wasn't ready to feel like a walking science project. A human pin cushion. For my body to stop feeling like mine and start feeling like a lab experiment with mood swings.

Eventually, we stopped trying. Not because we stopped wanting, but because I couldn't take the emotional whiplash anymore. Every month felt like a game of roulette, and every negative test felt like another silent little funeral.

Then came the guilt.

I cried. A lot. I cried at baby announcements. I cried walking past the baby aisle in Target. I cried when friends got pregnant; then wiped my tears, bought the bougiest diaper bag I could find, and showed up to the baby shower with a smile big enough to hide the ache.

Because I truly *was* happy for them. I loved watching my friends become moms. But I hated how it hollowed me out on the inside.

Here's the part that took me years to admit. I don't think I ever really wanted to be a mom.

I wanted to want it. I thought I *should* want it. I thought it was the natural next step, the one that would make me whole, make my marriage stronger, give my life some sort of ultimate meaning.

But that wasn't the truth. That was conditioning. Pressure. Timeline envy.

And life? Life had other plans. My husband, who, let's be honest, was not father-of-the-year material, left. And though it wrecked me in the moment, now I see the divine gift in the timing. I wasn't left holding the emotional baggage *and* a literal diaper bag.

(Nothing but absolute respect for single moms. I would lay down in traffic for you.)

Then COVID hit. Suddenly, my group chats turned into homeschool war zones. Everyone was crying over math and rationing Goldfish like wartime soldiers. And there I was Googling "what the hell is long division" just so I could text moral support.

That's when it hit me: this life was never for me. Not because I'm incapable. Not because I'm heartless. Not because I wouldn't be the most amazing mother. But because deep down, I'm already mothering the people I'm meant to. Just not in the way I thought I would.

I've got nieces. Nephews. Friend's kids. Honorary godchildren. A whole chaotic squad of tiny humans who see me as the fun one. The wild one. The one who brings glitter slime, messy art projects, dance parties, and endless snacks.

I'm not their mom; I'm their soft place to land. The bonus grown-up who always shows up.

I am the fun aunt. The fierce protector. The birthday hype squad. The person who answers the phone when they're scared to call their parents.

And that? That is *everything*.

Maybe I didn't get what I thought I wanted. But I got something just as meaningful: a role I was *actually* made for. A life that makes sense in ways I never expected. And the freedom to know I don't have to fulfill some outdated narrative to be whole.

For Anyone Who Thought "Mother" Was the Only Badge That Mattered

You are still whole. Still worthy. Still overflowing with love. Whether you have babies, bonus kids, fur children, plants that refuse to die, or none of the above, you are still a nurturer.

There is no one way to love. No checklist required. Your care, your presence, your heart? They matter. So, whether you're in the middle of trying, healing from the trying, or realizing you were never meant to try at all, this is your reminder:

You are enough. You are complete. You are allowed to want something different. And you are still *so damn needed.*

I'm not flaking. I'm just
emotionally booked and
socially bankrupt.

Chapter 14:

Anxious, Party of One.

The anxiety origin story nobody asked for, but here we are.

I used to think my anxiety showed up in adulthood. Like it waited until I had a mortgage, a broken marriage, and a pile of unread emails to sneak in and ruin the party. Like it RSVP'd late to my life and then just…never left. But the truth? It's been with me for as long as I can remember. It didn't show up in adulthood. It just got louder.

When I was little, I'd ask my mom nearly every day, *"Who's your favorite red headed daughter?"*

Now, in theory, this was a joke. Because duh, I was her *only* red headed daughter. But I needed to hear it. Not once. Not every so often. Every. Single. Day. People would roll their eyes or laugh it off, but I wasn't fishing for compliments. That was anxiety, dressed up in a silly little question. That was tiny-me begging for reassurance like it was oxygen. I didn't want to be *the favorite*, I just needed to feel seen. Needed to feel safe. Needed the validation that my brain wouldn't naturally offer.

Looking back, I see it now. That desperate need for constant affirmations wasn't about attention. It was about survival. It was about a brain wired to search for danger and rejection, even in the most loving places. I just didn't have the language for it back then. All I had were instincts that told me something felt off inside. Like I was built without the part that trusts good things.

And that? That was just the opening act.

Somewhere along the way, anxiety brought OCD to the party. Or maybe it was the other way around. Who knows. I just know that suddenly, I had thoughts that didn't belong to me; ones that barged in, set up shop, and refused to leave. Intrusive thoughts aren't just "weird" or "quirky." They're terrifying. They show up uninvited and say things like: *"If you don't flip that light switch again, your whole family is going to die."*

Excuse me?? What kind of mentally unhinged logic is that?

But I believed it. Not with my rational brain, but with my anxious, terrified one. So, I flipped the switch. Twice. Three times. Ten. Every single time. Because what if? What if I *didn't* and something awful happened? I knew it didn't make sense, but the fear didn't care.

Then depression entered like the grumpy cousin no one invited, dragging a suitcase full of hopelessness and apathy. In my early twenties, I didn't think depression was real. I thought it was a mood. A bad day. Something people could snap out of with enough motivation or caffeine. I cringe admitting that now, but I believed it. I genuinely thought people were just weak or too emotional.

And then? Life laughed and hit me with a tidal wave of darkness I couldn't outrun. Depression didn't knock, it just showed up and made itself at home. Suddenly, everything was heavy. Breathing. Showering. Answering texts. Existing. It was like my body kept moving while my mind disappeared. It wasn't sadness, it was nothingness. And I'd never felt more afraid.

I look back now and laugh at how clueless I was. But mostly, I give myself grace. We don't know what we don't know, and I didn't know shit. We're all just trying to figure it out with whatever tools we've got. And sometimes? We're working with broken ones and a blindfold. But we keep going.

Now? I manage it all, anxiety, OCD, depression, ADHD (because why stop at one diagnosis when you can collect the whole set?), with medication, self-work, and a lot of deep breaths. Some days are still hard. But they're no longer impossible. I've built a toolbox. I've learned my patterns. I've stopped shaming myself for needing help.

And I'll say it loud for the people in the back: Medication saved my damn life. Not made it easier. Not numbed me out. *Saved* it.

If you're scared of it? I get it. If you've been told you should be able to "handle it naturally," same. But please, please, please, don't write it off. Don't let stigma stand between you and your peace.

You deserve peace. You deserve relief. You deserve to not feel like a prisoner in your own mind.

And most of all, you deserve to feel like yourself again, maybe for the first time ever.

For Anyone Who's Been Told to "Just Calm Down"

That constant need for reassurance? That wasn't you being needy. That was your nervous system waving a bright red flag.

The overthinking? The soul-deep exhaustion after a five-minute conversation? Those weren't quirks. They were quiet cries for help that went unheard for way too long.

That anxious version of you, the one who cancels plans last minute, who over-packs for a day trip "just in case," who triple-checks the door, the stove, the iron, and the damn garage door? She's not crazy. She's been in survival mode for years.

She doesn't need shame. She needs compassion.

Give yourself the same grace you offer to everyone else. Wrap yourself in gentleness. In patience. In reminders that healing isn't some perfect, Pinterest-ready transformation. It's messy. It's nonlinear. And it counts even on the days when you feel like a human question mark.

You are not too much. You are not broken. You are doing your best.

And that is more than enough.

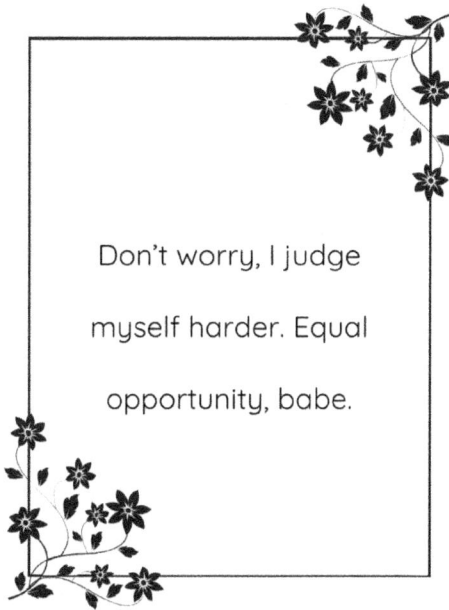

Don't worry, I judge

myself harder. Equal

opportunity, babe.

Chapter 15:

Judgy Since Birth

Hi, I'm Carrie, and I've been mentally side-eyeing since 1970-something.

Let's be honest. Sometimes I judge people for the dumbest things. The shoes they paired with that outfit. The way they spell *definitely* like *definately*. The fact that they said *expresso* instead of *espresso*. (WHY. Like, there is no "x" in that word, sweetie. None.) I'll be scrolling, side-eyeing, sipping my coffee with a silent monologue like I'm running a one-woman fashion-police-meets-spell-check reality show.

The older I get, the more I've realized something uncomfortable: The things I judge the hardest? Are usually the things I'm secretly judging in *myself*. Oof. It's like a little mirror shows up every time I cringe at someone's choices, and surprise, it's actually pointed at me.

I've learned that judgment can feel like control. Like safety. If I can pick people apart, I don't have to sit with my own insecurities. I can stay above it. Detached. Unbothered.

But that's just a trick of the ego. It's not real power, it's projection.

In the past several years, I've been trying to "be a better person" (Whatever that means. Less petty? More evolved? Fewer unnecessary roasts?). And one rule that's actually helped me is this:

If they can't change it in 5 seconds, keep your mouth shut.

Spinach in teeth? Okay, say something. Their weight, their laugh, their entire existence? Not your damn business. Sometimes though, even if I don't *say* it out loud, the thought pops in. That snarky, smug little inner voice that wants to offer unsolicited commentary like I'm on a panel for *America's Next Top Personal Failure.*

What do I do? I try to let that thought drift away. Evaporate into the guilt cloud that lives rent-free in my brain. The one that whispers, "You know better now. Try again next time." Because awareness doesn't mean perfection. It just means catching yourself when your brain starts handing out gold medals in the Judgement Olympics.

I was raised in a judgy world.

Aunts who could weaponize an eyebrow raise. Family gatherings that turned into passive-aggressive roast sessions. Someone's outfit? Their job? Their dating choices? Fair game. And if you dared date one of the male cousins in our family? Good fucking luck. You were walking into a firing squad armed with lipstick, pursed lips, and sweet tea full of secrets.

To them, it wasn't cruelty. It was sport. It was bonding. It was, dare I say…tradition.

I didn't question it until I got old enough to be judged myself. To hear the whispers as I left the room. To feel the sting of knowing someone else had passed a verdict on me based on half the story and none of the truth. That's when it clicked: *This isn't who I want to be.* I didn't want my legacy to be the human version of a Yelp review no one asked for.

Now? I try to lead with curiosity instead of criticism. When I catch myself about to judge, I pause and ask, *"What does this say about me?"* Most of the time, the answer isn't pretty. But it's honest. And it reminds me that I'm not above anyone. I'm just trying, like everyone else, to get through the day with a shred of dignity and maybe a decent meal.

People are already fighting battles we'll never see. They're carrying invisible things like grief, trauma, mental illness, the weight of just being human. And honestly? I've got enough of my own shit to sort through. I don't have time to audit theirs. My energy is better spent unpacking my own baggage, not dragging someone else's into the spotlight for sport.

If you see me biting my tongue, taking a breath, and choosing empathy over shade? That's growth. Not perfection. Just progress.

One unspoken judgment at a time.

For Anyone Still Learning to Lead with Grace Instead of Judgment

Judgment is easy. Safe. It makes us feel superior without asking us to do any of the messy emotional labor. But here's the truth bomb: most of the time, judgment isn't about them, it's about *us*. It's projection dressed up as opinion. A mirror we didn't ask to look into, reflecting every part of ourselves we haven't made peace with yet.

Before you roll your eyes at someone's choices, ask yourself: Is this really about *them*, or is it poking at something I haven't healed in myself?

We don't talk enough about how judgment can become armor, a way to avoid vulnerability, to dodge our own discomfort. But growth? Growth is setting that armor down, one snarky thought at a time. It's pausing before you speak. It's calling yourself out with love, not shame.

And when you slip (because you *will* slip), remember this: slipping doesn't mean starting over. It just means you're human. Self-awareness is the win. Accountability is the power move. Compassion is the transformation.

You don't have to be perfect. You just have to keep choosing better; even if it takes 1,000 tries. That version of you who used to judge out of habit? She deserves grace too. She was trying to survive.

But the you now? You're not surviving anymore. You're evolving.

And evolution looks damn good on you.

I don't do secrets. I do
uncomfortable truths with a
side of nervous laughter.

Chapter 16:
My Trauma Just Jumped Out Mid-Conversation

When my "normal" childhood stories clear a room real fast.

Up until about ten years ago, I would've never used the word *trauma* to describe my childhood.

I mean, I was born a white woman in Dallas, Texas. That alone comes with plenty of privilege. I wasn't dodging bombs or growing up in extreme poverty. I had food, shelter, a school to go to, and parents who *technically* showed up. The only thing that would've made it more privileged is if I'd popped out as a white man…but let's not even go there. I grew up thinking trauma had to be big, bold, headline-worthy. Something worthy of a Lifetime movie. What it actually looks like sometimes is just…life.

The shift came when I started talking. Really talking. Not just the surface-level, laugh-it-off kind of sharing, but the *let me tell you what actually happened and hope you don't look at me differently afterward* kind of talking. I'd casually drop some story at a dinner table full of friends, some moment from my childhood I thought was just another Tuesday, and then…silence. You know that kind of silence where everyone stops chewing, forks mid-air, and they all just *stare* at you like you accidentally announced you were raised by wolves? Yeah. That one.

That's when I realized: Oh. This isn't everyone's experience. This wasn't normal. This was trauma just wrapped in different packaging.

Because trauma doesn't always announce itself with sirens. It's not always about assault, or violence, or catastrophe. Sometimes it's chronic. Subtle. Repetitive. It slips in quietly, wearing a friendly face and carrying phrases like "this is just how we do things." It's the yelling you normalized. The love you had to earn. The manipulation buried under *"I'm just trying to help."* The emotional neglect disguised as "tough love." The worst part? You thought everyone else had the same thing. You thought it was just *life*.

It took years for me to even consider using the word *trauma* without immediately feeling guilty or dramatic. I'd downplay my story in my head before anyone else could: "It wasn't that bad," "Other people have had it worse," "At least they didn't…" But that's the trick trauma plays. It convinces you it wasn't real because it didn't look like someone else's pain.

Here's what I know now: My mom did the best she could. She raised me with what she had; financially, emotionally, spiritually. She wasn't perfect, and neither was the environment I grew up in, but I genuinely believe she loved me. And even though there were hard, confusing, holy-shit moments, I wouldn't change it. Because those moments made me who I am today: kind, loyal, hyper-aware, strong as hell…and absolutely *done* letting people walk all over me.

I don't need to rewrite the past to honor my present. I can love where I came from and still be honest about what hurt. That's not betrayal, it's healing. It's truth. It's me finally stepping into my story without editing it to protect someone else's comfort.

If you're holding something in, something that feels too weird, too heavy, too messy, say it out loud. Not to the whole world. Maybe just to one person. A friend. A therapist. Someone who won't flinch when they hear your truth. Someone who will look at you and say, *"That makes sense. You make sense."*

Because sometimes, getting it out is the first step in realizing: It wasn't your shame to carry.

It was something that *happened to you*. And it is absolutely, unequivocally, not your fault.

For Anyone Who's Minimized Their Pain Into Silence

Sometimes the scariest things we say out loud are the ones we never even thought *were* traumatic until we saw the way someone else reacted to them. That "oh" moment when your story lands like a grenade at a dinner table.

That's when it hits: Your "normal" might've been anything *but*.

Trauma isn't always loud. Sometimes it's quiet. Consistent. Buried in moments you tried to brush off.

Acknowledging it? That's liberation. Saying it out loud can feel terrifying, like taking off armor you didn't realize you'd been wearing for decades. When you say the scary thing, you start to realize how much of your story deserves *compassion*, not judgment.

If you've been carrying something heavy, quietly convincing yourself it "wasn't a big deal" ...Maybe today's the day. Say it to someone safe. Say it to *yourself*.

You don't have to shout it. But you *don't* have to carry it alone anymore. That weight? It was never meant to be yours forever.

Rest isn't laziness. It's me surviving this hellscape with snacks and minimal interaction.

Chapter 17:

Mentally Ill, Hella Aware, and Chronically Done

aka: The Bed Is My Safe Space, Mind Your Business

Growing up, I always felt…different. Bigger feelings. Louder thoughts. Deeper worries. I didn't have the words for it back then; I just knew my brain was doing the absolute *most* at all times. While other kids seemed to coast, I was either stuck in overdrive or parked in neutral, staring at the wall wondering why everything felt like *too much*. Noise? Too much. Group projects? Too much. Existential dread at age seven? Also, too much.

I thought I was dramatic. I thought I was broken. I thought I was just *bad* at being a person. But what I really was? Unseen. Unnamed. Unexplained.

Fast-forward a few decades (and a handful of mental health diagnoses), and surprise: I've got a whole party happening in my head! ADHD, OCD, depression, anxiety. And just to keep things spicy, I'm also an empath. As if I needed an extra emotional side quest. It's not a personality type. It's not a vibe. It's a full-body experience of feeling every single emotion in the room like I *ordered it myself*.

When you get all this information as an adult, it's like someone finally hands you the missing script to a play you've been awkwardly improvising your whole damn life. Suddenly, everything clicks. Like puzzle pieces that were hiding under the couch cushions of your childhood.

Why I hated school.

Why I couldn't focus unless I was hyper-fixated or completely panicked.

Why I cried during commercials.

Why I couldn't stop overthinking things that happened years ago.

Why I had intrusive thoughts that made me question my own sanity.

Why I could feel someone else's pain like it had a forwarding address to my nervous system.

Why loud spaces, big emotions, and high-speed expectations made me want to hide under a blanket.

I wasn't lazy. I wasn't dramatic. I wasn't "too sensitive." I was *unmedicated, misunderstood,* and completely drowning in neurodivergence in a world built for structure, schedules, and silence. A world that rewards the calm, the controlled, the convenient, and punishes anyone who colors outside the lines.

These days? I've reclaimed the hell out of my healing. And with that, I have fallen in love my bed. I *worship* my bed. I *need* my bed.

It's not just a comfort item; it's my reset zone. My sanctuary. The only damn place in my world that doesn't demand more from me than I have to give. No expectations. No pressure. No emotional downloads. Just blankets, silence, and a return to baseline.

People love to joke and call it lazy. Like rest is optional. Like stillness is weakness. But they don't see what it takes for me to function. To be "on" all day, masking every feeling, carrying everyone else's energy while trying not to drown in your own. They don't see the exhaustion behind the eye rolls. The effort behind the "I'm fine."

I don't choose stillness because I'm lazy. I choose it because it's how I *stay alive*. It's how I recharge after moving through a world that often feels like sensory assault and emotional gymnastics.

And honestly? Y'all should try it sometime. Sacred rest is for the cool kids. Give it a chance. Cancel those plans. Turn off the group chat. Treat your peace like it's your last fuck. If you've only got one left, don't waste it.

For Anyone Who's Been Called Lazy When They Were Actually Just Overwhelmed

If your bed is your sanctuary, your quiet time is non-negotiable, and your energy runs out faster than your to-do list, you are not alone. And more importantly? You are not broken.

You are navigating a world that demands 24/7 productivity while your brain is screaming for pause. You are decoding social cues, filtering noise, managing overstimulation, and trying to meet deadlines with executive dysfunction nipping at your heels. That's not laziness. That's endurance.

Stop apologizing for needing rest. Stop explaining why you didn't RSVP, show up, or text back right away. You are not a machine. You are a human being with limits, and recognizing those limits is a *superpower*, not a flaw.

You are allowed to choose your peace over other people's pressure.

You're allowed to take up space *and* take a nap.

You're allowed to say "no" without a dissertation on your mental state.

Rest isn't a luxury. It isn't indulgent. It's survival.

Rest isn't weakness. It's an act of self-preservation.

Protect it like your life depends on it.

Because sometimes, it kind of does.

Chapter 18:
Burnout Isn't a Personality Trait

You can't pour from an empty cup. I tried but just ended up throwing the damn cup.

Let's get something straight right off the top: self-care is not a luxury. It's not selfish. It's not optional. It's *essential*. It's the thing you do so you don't absolutely lose your damn mind trying to be everything for everyone, every single day.

Because when life feels like a never-ending group project where everyone expects you to carry weight, but no one else is even holding a pencil, you need to take a step back, breathe, and remember this: *You. Come. First.*

Etch this into your soul, sweetheart.

YOU. COME. FIRST.

When the world makes you feel like you're drowning, no, a bubble bath won't save your life. It won't fix generational trauma or pay your bills. But you know what it *can* do? Make your night 10% more tolerable. And sometimes that's enough. Sometimes, that's the win.

Self-care isn't just about candles and skincare routines (though yes, for the love of God, light the damn candle). It's about preserving your energy. Protecting your peace. Creating moments, no matter how small, are just for *you*. It's drinking your coffee while it's still hot. It's closing your door and blasting Reputation for four straight minutes. It's saying no without explaining yourself. It's choosing to refill *your* tank before you run out of gas and end up broken down on the side of your own life.

Let's talk about the guilt. Oh, the *guilt*. That creeping little voice whispering, "You should be with the kids." "Shouldn't you be doing something productive?" No, babe. *You're being productive by staying sane.*

Dropping your kids off to get a workout in? Not selfish.

Enjoying a quiet dinner with your husband? Not neglectful.

Getting wine-drunk and screaming-laughing with your girlfriends on a random Wednesday? Not irresponsible.

That's called balance. That's called living. That's called *being human.*

Women, especially mothers, have been spoon-fed this lie that if we're not suffering, we're not doing it right. If we're not exhausted, we're not enough. If we're not drowning in everyone else's needs, we're failing. To that I say *absolutely not.*

Taking care of yourself does not make you a bad mother. It makes you a *better* one. A more patient one. A more present one. Same goes for being a friend, a daughter, a partner, an employee. You can't show up for everyone else while constantly ghosting yourself.

Let's break the cycle! You don't have to earn rest. You don't have to apologize for peace. You don't need permission to prioritize yourself.

Because here's the thing. If you don't take care of you, no one else is going to magically step in and do it. No one's handing out medals for martyrdom. You don't get a cookie for burning out. But you *do* get resentment. You do get fatigue. And you do get breakdowns in grocery store parking lots because you haven't had a minute to just *be.*

Start choosing you. Hell, schedule it in if you have to. Self-care isn't a backup plan. It's the foundation. You wouldn't skip an oil change and expect your car to keep running. Why the hell do you think your body, your brain, your soul can go without maintenance?

Give yourself what you need. Silence. Movement. Joy. Solitude. Sleep. Therapy. Time with the people who refill you instead of drain you. Create boundaries like your life depends on it, because spoiler alert: it does.

For Anyone Who's Been Told Putting Themselves First is Selfish

Taking care of yourself is how you stay soft in a world that keeps trying to harden you.

You are not a machine. You are not here to serve and sacrifice until there's nothing left of you but a smile and a to-do list. You're allowed to pause. You're allowed to take a break. And you're allowed to make yourself the priority, no justification needed.

Self-care isn't just a moment of peace; it's an act of resistance. It's how we protect our joy, preserve our energy, and remind ourselves that we are not just background characters in everyone else's life. You get to be the main character in your own life. That means rest. That means pleasure. That means choosing yourself even when it's inconvenient for others.

The next time you feel guilty for doing something that fills your cup, ask yourself this: Who benefits when I'm running on empty? Because it sure as hell isn't you. You matter. You're needed. But you're also *deserving*; of joy, of rest, of love, and of every damn bubble bath you want to take.

I inherited a round face and body shame. One I'll contour, the other I'm unlearning.

Chapter 19:
Body by Generational Trauma

This isn't body positivity, it's survival with a side of shame.

The women before me hated their bodies and called it discipline. I'm calling it what it is: inherited self-loathing wrapped in sugar-free yogurt and shame.

I don't remember a time when the women around me *weren't* at war with their bodies. It wasn't always loud. It wasn't always obvious. But it was constant.

In my family, your worth was often measured in dress sizes and complemented in pounds lost. Someone's success was validated by a "Wow, you look so thin!" Someone's failure? A quiet whisper about how "she's really let herself go." Even my own grandmother would call out my weight gain before she even said hi.

The women I grew up around were always on a new diet. Atkins, keto, Weight Watchers, South Beach, cabbage soup, Slim Fast, grapefruit for breakfast and guilt for dessert. Their routines changed, but the mission stayed the same: shrink. Be smaller. Be less.

Someone was always trying to shrink. Their bodies. Their appetites. Their presence.

And whether they realized it or not, I was watching. Listening. Absorbing every calorie-counting, fat-shaming, self-loathing comment like it was gospel. Their shame was a family heirloom, wrapped in concern and passed down with good intentions and terrible consequences.

We all fluctuated. Up five, down ten. Celebrating one day, hiding from cameras the next.

Fasting before the reunion. Sucking in for photos. Pinching at "problem areas" in the mirror.

And no one ever questioned it, because that's just what women did. That's what being female was supposed to look like: a lifelong apology for the space you take up.

We hated our thighs. We skipped the bread. We bonded over how "bad" we'd been for eating pasta. We called ourselves "good" when we were hungry and "gross" when we were full. We weren't nourishing ourselves; we were performing obedience. It was normal. Except…it *wasn't*.

There's a voice memo on Avery Anna's album called "My Mother Lies." She talks about how she listens to her mom criticize her own body every day, and she looks exactly like her. When she says, *"my mother lies,"* I felt it in my chest. Because I've lived that lyric. I've been that girl.

When my mom tells me I'm beautiful all I think is: *How could I be, if you're not?* We literally look exactly the same! How could I believe you when you praise me but loathe the body I came from?

That disconnect doesn't disappear with compliments. It seeps into your bones. It becomes the voice inside your own head. The voice that whispers in fitting rooms, critiques your reflection in windows, and convinces you that your body is a problem to be fixed, not a place you can simply live in.

And no matter how body-positive the world *pretends* to be now, those early messages? They're sticky as hell. They don't leave just because you follow a few plus-size influencers or buy the jeans with the stretchy waistband. They've been living rent-free in your head for decades, rearranging the furniture of your self-worth.

What I have begun to realize is, I don't owe anyone thinness. I don't owe them progress pics, calorie logs, or before-and-afters. I don't owe them the illusion that I'm okay in a body I was taught to hate.

What I owe *myself* is compassion. Rest. Comfort. Permission to exist without commentary. To eat a damn sandwich without shame. To wear the shorts. To be in the photo. To stop treating my body like a PR campaign.

My body is not a problem to solve. It is not a project to fix. It is not up for public debate.

It's just mine.

For Anyone Still Carrying Inherited Shame in Their Skin

If the women before you hated their bodies, how could you ever learn to love yours?

This isn't just about weight. It's about *legacy*. It's about the invisible curriculum we absorbed from the women we loved most. Lessons we never asked for but learned anyway.

It's what gets passed down without words: Through mirror glances. Through skipped meals. Through "I can't believe I ate that" like it's a confession. Through dessert skipped like it's a character trait. Through joy filtered through guilt.

But hear this: The cycle can stop with you.

You do *not* have to carry this shame one step further. You do *not* have to speak the language of self-loathing just because it was your first dialect. You don't have to keep living under the rules written by someone else's insecurity.

Hand it back. Not with bitterness, but with healing. Let it end with you. You deserve to live in your body without apology. To take up space. To *like yourself* on purpose. To feed your body without explaining why it's allowed to eat.

You were never too much. Your body was never the problem. And loving yourself loudly? That's the revolution.

Let them call it radical. Let them call it delusional. You just keep calling it *freedom*.

Self-worth isn't
arrogance. It's
survival in a world
built to dim you.

Chapter 20:

I'm Not Arrogant. I'm Just Aware of My Power.

Loving myself isn't the problem. It's your fragile ego that can't handle my confidence.

Here's something that might surprise you: I've always loved myself.

Like, genuinely. Deeply. Unapologetically. Not in a performative, hashtag-affirmation kind of way, but in a soul-level knowing that I was built with purpose. That I belong here. That I matter. Even when the world tried to convince me otherwise.

Now, don't get it twisted. I'm not walking around thinking I'm better than anyone else. This isn't ego, it's essence. I've never believed I was perfect. But I've always believed I was *worthy*. Worthy of love. Of space. Of peace. Of joy that didn't have to be earned. Of softness that didn't have to be explained.

And apparently…that's a crazy thing for a woman to admit out loud.

Because in the world I grew up in, loving yourself out loud was a threat. It meant you were conceited. Vain. "Full of yourself." And if there's one thing patriarchy hates, it's a woman who doesn't need outside validation to feel powerful.

Meanwhile, I was just trying to exist in peace with the body, brain, and soul I was given. I wasn't trying to be better than anyone else, I was just trying to be *me* without apology. Without shrinking. Without dimming my light because it made someone else squint.

I never claimed to be perfect. I was just…mine. Fully, completely, divinely mine. Made exactly how I was meant to be. And last I checked, God doesn't do accidents.

The wildest part? I have no idea where that self-assurance came from. Because I didn't learn it by example.

Most of the women around me picked themselves apart like it was their second job. Every wrinkle. Every pound. Every laugh line that dared to show up without permission. They saw flaws where I saw *human*. And somehow, my refusal to hate myself made them uncomfortable.

But here's the truth: I wasn't the problem. *Their* discomfort was.

Yes, I've been in bad relationships. Controlling ones. Emotionally manipulative ones. I've been gaslit, guilt-tripped, underestimated, shut down. I've let people take more from me than I should've allowed. I've bent, broken, and contorted myself into shapes I didn't recognize, all in the name of love, approval, belonging.

But not once - not *once* - did I stop loving myself.

Even at my lowest. Even when I ignored red flags. Even when I betrayed my own boundaries just to keep the peace. Some small, fierce part of me always whispered, *"This isn't where it ends. You are worth more than this."*

That love for myself?

It's what pulled me out of every mess I got thrown into...*or threw myself into*. It's what lit the way back when everything felt dark. It's what made me rebuild, reset, and rise again every single time.

And now? The tides are finally turning.

We are stepping into an era where women are reclaiming their bodies, their beauty, their voices. Where self-love is no longer taboo, it's power. Where we're allowed to be proud, soft, strong, sexy, messy, opinionated, sensitive, assertive, healing, *and whole*, as we are. No edits. No explanations.

And let me tell you. It's about damn time.

If my self-love makes people uneasy? Good. Let them shift in their seat. Let them sit with their discomfort while I sit in my worth.

Because I'm not shrinking for anyone. Not now. Not ever.

For Anyone Who's Been Told Their Self-Love Was Too Loud

Loving yourself in a world that profits from your insecurity is not arrogance, it's *survival*. It's resistance. It's the softest rebellion and the loudest revolution.

You weren't born to beg for approval. You weren't built to edit yourself for someone else's comfort. You weren't put here to shrink, apologize, or wait your turn.

You were born to take up space, with your full laugh, your loud opinions, your soft heart, and your fierce boundaries.

You are allowed to root for yourself. Out loud. Without disclaimers.

If no one ever told you this: It's not vain to love yourself. It's *revolutionary*. Especially when you've survived relationships, systems, and environments that tried to convince you otherwise.

Stand tall in your self-love. Not just the polished, filtered parts, but the messy, raw, still-learning, still-growing, still-healing parts, too.

Because that kind of love? That's the kind that heals generations.

Let them call it too loud. You just keep calling it *home*.

Grief said I'd never smile again.
I said watch me, bitch.

Chapter 21:
Grief Is a Lying Bastard

Healing isn't linear. It's a bitch in heels with bad timing.

They say grief comes in stages: denial, anger, bargaining, depression, acceptance.

Cute chart.

In my experience, grief doesn't follow rules. It doesn't give you space to recover or time to prepare. It shows up like a wrecking ball during brunch and refuses to leave, even when you've vacuumed, saged the place, and lit a candle.

I thought I knew grief. I'd had moments. But nothing prepared me for the six-year grief marathon I didn't sign up for.

It started with my dog. And no, I don't need anyone to tell me, "He was just a dog." He was family. He was comfort. He was there when people failed me. And when he died, I cried like my chest had been cracked wide open. That kind of love doesn't just come with fur, it comes with soul ties. And his were wrapped all over mine.

Then I lost one of my work "dads", a coworker turned friend turned protector. The kind of man who shows up, checks in, and quietly becomes part of your everyday safety net. When he died, it felt like the world shifted slightly off its axis. I still catch myself *every single day* reaching for things I want to tell him.

Then came the divorce. One I didn't ask for. Didn't want. Didn't agree with at the time. It felt like failure, rejection, and an identity crisis all wrapped in legal paperwork. Looking back (see Chapter 10 for the rebrand), I know now it was a gift. But back then? It was heartbreak in real time.

The hits kept coming.

My cousin died in a car accident. Gone too fast, too young, too unfair. There was no time to process, just shock and the sound of family fracturing in the background.

Shortly before his accident, my aunt was diagnosed with a brain tumor. Watching someone you love fade slowly is its own kind of torture. You start grieving long before they're gone.

And right after her passing? Half of my mom's family disowned us. A dumb fight about a wedding turned into complete silence. Abandoned by people who once shared my birthday cake. That grief is layered: loss mixed with rejection, soaked in bitterness.

And then…there was him. One of the great loves of my life. The kind you write songs about. Or create a dramatic podcast series for. His death? Suspicious at best. Tragic at worst. It still doesn't make sense. Maybe it never will. That kind of grief comes with questions no one's willing to answer. And it lingers long after the condolences stop.

Those six years of hell didn't just leave bruises, they rewired me. I came out of the other side with depression, anxiety, and a nervous system that flinched at the sound of my own thoughts. I don't know how to function without crisis. I don't know who I am without grief as my co-pilot.

I am surviving, sure. But thriving? That feels like a foreign concept. It takes everything in me not to shut down completely. Grief didn't just take people I loved; it took parts of me I'm still trying to get back.

For Anyone That Has Been Shattered by Grief

Grief is a liar.

It tells you the pain will never fade. That you're stuck. That you'll always feel like this. It whispers that the world has moved on without you, and maybe you should, too. That joy is a place you'll never get back to. That healing is betrayal. That smiling means forgetting. That laughter makes you ungrateful for what you lost.

But grief is also a teacher. Ruthless. Sharp. Honest in ways that tear you open.

It doesn't come with a syllabus. No timeline. No "how to." It arrives unannounced, rips the floor out from under you, and dares you to build something new in its place. It shows up in waves and wreckage, in silence and screams, and in the smallest moments, like a scent, a song, or a random Tuesday that brings you to your knees.

And still, through the wreckage, it teaches you how to love deeper. How to let go softer. How to hold memories like fragile glass, gently, reverently, without cutting yourself every time.

It teaches that some people never leave us, not really. That "moving on" is a myth, but *moving forward* with them woven into your story is possible. That presence doesn't always require a body. That legacy can live in laughter, in traditions, in the way you carry kindness like they did.

Grief also teaches you that healing and hurting can sit at the same table. That you can cry while laughing. That you can miss someone fiercely and still find joy again, not because you're over it, but because you've made peace with carrying it.

That joy and pain aren't opposites, they're roommates. Unlikely ones, but roommates nonetheless.

There is no right way to grieve. No checklist. No magic number of days. But every time I tell a story about them, every time I light a candle, play their favorite song, or simply pause to feel it all, I heal.

Just a little. Just enough.

And sometimes, that's enough for one day. And if it's not? Then just breathing is. Because even in the silence, you're still moving. Even in the ache, you're still honoring. And even in the darkest grief, you are still deeply, unmistakably *alive*.

Plot twist: I don't need
your blessing to live
my loud little life.

Chapter 22:
If It Makes You Happy, Who the Hell Cares?

Politics, religion, sexuality: the unholy trinity of things people love to argue about at a dinner table.

Bring up any of them, and suddenly your uncle is sweating, your cousin's clenching her jaw, and your grandma is whispering a prayer into her mashed potatoes. It's wild how fast a room can go from talking about football to threatening to disown each other over who someone voted for in 2016.

We live in a world where everything feels like a fight. Every post. Every policy. Every commercial. Every damn dinner table.

It's exhausting to simply exist with your own beliefs, especially when those beliefs don't fit neatly into the boxes other people believe are "right." The second you challenge the narrative, suddenly you're "radical," "aggressive," or "trying to start something."

When really? You're just existing. Breathing. Speaking up. Living your truth in a world that demands your silence.

I live in a conservative state, surrounded by conservative coworkers, and come from a family tree with more elephants than a Republican convention. Cookouts feel like Fox News had a family reunion and forgot to tell MSNBC they weren't invited. And guess what?

I'm not conservative. Not even close.

I believe love is love. No disclaimers, no footnotes.

I believe Black lives matter. Not just in hashtags, but in policies, protection, and power.

I believe women should have full control over their bodies. Without apology, without explanation.

I believe religion should never be used as a weapon to control people or legislate morality.

I believe trans rights are human rights, and compassion should never be controversial.

I also curse. And have tattoos. I've had premarital sex and way too many existential crises. I exist in a body that people love to judge, from strangers on the internet to relatives at the reunion.

And I still sleep just fine at night.

Because none of those things define how kind, honest, or empathetic I am. None of those things determine whether I show up for my friends, check on my neighbors, or give a damn about people who don't look, live, or love like me.

I show up. I care. I try. And that, to me, is what actually matters.

It's scary to speak up when you're surrounded by people who think differently, especially when those people are your coworkers, your community, or your own damn family.

But silence? That's not me.

And if it's not you either, then say it. Say it scared. Say it tired. Say it even when your voice shakes and your hands are sweating and your heart feels like it's doing burpees.

Because the truth is, silence doesn't keep the peace. It just maintains the comfort of people who already feel safe. It protects power, not people. And I'm not here for that.

You don't have to be perfect. You don't have to have a debate team resume or a TED Talk script. You just have to be real. Honest. Open-hearted. Willing to stand in the uncomfortable truth that some people won't like you simply because you think differently.

Above all else though, be kind.

Believe what you believe. Stand in it. Live it. But don't tear others down for doing the same. Be firm without being cruel. Be passionate without being condescending. Because kindness doesn't mean silence, and compassion doesn't mean compliance.

We're not here long. Don't waste your life trying to win arguments with people who have already decided they're right. You don't need to prove yourself in every room. You just need to *be* yourself.

Spend your energy building a life you're proud of. One that reflects your values, not your fear. One that feels like truth, not performance.

And love others loud enough to drown out the noise. Because that's the kind of legacy that actually matters.

For Anyone Not Living in Their Truth

What do you believe in when no one's watching?
What opinions do you silence at dinner to keep the peace?
What truths do you swallow so you don't rock the boat?
What parts of yourself do you keep hidden because they don't match the version of you that others have decided is "acceptable"?

It's easy to go quiet in rooms full of loud opinions. Especially when they come wrapped in tradition. Tied with family ties. Backed by fear and familiarity.

But here's the truth. Your values matter. Your voice matters. And being a good person has *nothing* to do with how quietly you blend in. It's about how boldly and compassionately you show up, even when it's uncomfortable. Even when it costs you something. Even when it makes the room shift and your hands shake.

Ask yourself. *Really* ask: Am I living my truth? Or the version that's easiest for others to accept?

Write it out. Say it out loud. Speak it into the mirror, even if no one else is listening yet.

Because the world doesn't need more people playing it safe. It doesn't need more approval-seekers or peacekeepers or people-pleasers. It needs more people brave enough to be kind without being quiet. To love without limits. To show up with honesty and lead with empathy. To say, "This is what I believe," and stand tall even when the ground shakes.

Take the risk. Rock the boat. Be the one who says the thing that needed to be said.

Because silence never changed the world. But truth? Spoken with love? That just might.

If loving your neighbor makes people
mad, they were never your people.

Chapter 23:

Whatever Happened to Just Not Being an Asshole?

Decency didn't die; it just got drowned in performative patriotism.

It seems like almost daily, I ask myself what happened to human decency?

Like…seriously. Did it quietly retire without a goodbye party? Did empathy and compassion just pack their bags and ghost the human race?

What happened to loving thy neighbor? Not "love them if they vote like you," or "love them if they were born within your imaginary borders," but just…*love them*. Period. Show up for them. Respect them. Care enough to not treat people like actual garbage because they don't fit your curated worldview.

The truth is, I miss the days when political differences didn't mean all-out war. Sure, we've always had opinions. We've voted differently, gone to different churches, raised our kids differently. But friendships didn't used to dissolve over Fox News vs. MSNBC. Families didn't cut each other off over vaccine memes. We didn't call people "evil" because they asked for basic human rights or god forbid *used a gender-neutral pronoun.*

Now? It's like empathy has been replaced with ego. If you say something like, "Hey, maybe we shouldn't treat immigrants like livestock in cages stacked 38-deep over an alligator swamp," suddenly you're "the problem." Or you get hit with the ever classic, "Well they shouldn't have come here illegally!"

First of all, most of them didn't. Most are in a hellish legal process that none of the people complaining could even *begin* to understand. And second of all…THEY'RE PEOPLE. Children. Families. Human beings who deserve better than Alligator Alcatraz.

When I point this out? I don't come at people sideways. I ask, "Okay, but why do you *disagree* with treating people with basic dignity?" I want to hear the real reason. Not the regurgitated Fox talking points. Not the "it's about the law" excuse. The real answer. Because sometimes, the truth is that they don't care. They lack empathy. And sometimes…they *might* be just a wee bit racist. Even if they wouldn't say that part out loud.

There's this idea people cling to that they're "not political." Oh babe, let's clear this up real quick: you don't have to be political to be decent. There's nothing radical about wanting people to have clean water, safe shelter, healthcare, and the ability to live without fear. That's not left or right. That's human.

Something I've started noticing, is that some people don't even *think* for themselves anymore. They parrot what their racist uncle said, or what their husband yells at the TV every night, or what their church has twisted into gospel. And they cling to it, not because it makes sense, but because it's easier than challenging their comfort zone.

Here's the thing though: your comfort zone might be someone else's hell. And if that makes you uncomfortable to hear? Good. Sit with it.

We've made it "controversial" to care. To give a damn. To say, "Hey, maybe trans kids deserve safety." "Hey, maybe black people shouldn't have to fear traffic stops." "Hey, maybe we could just…not be assholes today." And for some reason, when you say these things, *you're* the one accused of stirring the pot. No, babe. The pot was boiling hot long before I got here, I'm just calling it what it is.

I don't want to live in a world where silence is more polite than compassion. I don't want to raise the next generation to believe it's "political" to give a shit. If we want the world to get better, we have to stop treating empathy like a weakness. We have to start calling out people who use "free speech" as a shield for cruelty. And we have to stop defending hate because it came from someone we love.

You don't have to have a screaming match with your meemaw, but you *can* say, "That's not okay." You *can* unlearn things. You *can* hold people accountable with grace. And you *can* lead with compassion without compromising your backbone.

Because at the end of the day, decency didn't disappear. It just got buried under a whole lot of fear, pride, and echo chambers. And it's up to us to dig that shit out.

For Anyone Who's Been Told They're "Too Sensitive" for Caring About People

You're not too sensitive. The world's just gotten too comfortable being cruel.

If you've been the one speaking up in rooms that go silent, or worse, hostile, this chapter is for you. It takes real courage to hold onto your humanity in a world that rewards apathy. When everyone else is desensitized, it's easy to feel like you're the problem for giving a damn. But you are *not* the problem. You're the example.

Being decent shouldn't be revolutionary. But right now, it is. And the world needs more people who are willing to say, "Enough." Enough cruelty. Enough turning a blind eye. Enough excusing hate because it came from "nice people." Compassion doesn't make you weak, it makes you dangerous to a system built on silence.

Keep your empathy sharp. Use your voice. Question the bullshit, even when it's coming from someone you love. Decency isn't gone; it's just waiting on us to remember what it looks like. Let's bring it back with fire, grace, and a whole lot of unapologetic truth.

I'll just be over here laughing, thriving and not answering texts that ruin my vibe.

Chapter 24:
Live Loudly

Life's too short to shrink or settle. Especially for people who drain your soul.

As a kid, life was just…life. You played. You laughed. You existed without fear as your baseline. You weren't waiting for the other shoe to drop. You weren't rehearsing worst-case scenarios or scanning every moment for danger. You didn't have to think five steps ahead or brace for impact. Your world felt mostly safe, even if it wasn't perfect. Your job was to show up, eat snacks, and stay upright on your bike.

And then one day…it flips.

The phone rings in the middle of the night. Someone's crying. Someone's gone.

And suddenly, you're living in a world where anything can fall apart at any time. The safety you once took for granted? Gone. The people you thought were permanent? Not. And your body - your sweet, innocent nervous system - gets rewired to never fully relax again.

For me, that shift came around 2012, and I swear my brain cells haven't been the same since.

It was like a switch flipped and everything after it was colored in grayscale. Since then, I've spent years, *years*, waiting for the next wave to hit. I don't sleep well. I never have. What if I miss the call? What if I wake up to news that breaks me all over again?

Still, I don't turn my phone off. Not ever. Especially not at night. What if someone needs me? What if I'm the call they make, and I miss it? That's not just anxiety. That's *experience*. That's trauma with a memory and a timer and a ringtone. And it lingers long after the worst is over.

I think about the people who've purposely left my life, family, friends, people I thought were forever, who called it "boundaries" but used it like a trapdoor. Look, I get it. Boundaries can be beautiful. Healthy. Necessary. But they shouldn't be a substitute for hard conversations. They're not a mic drop. They're not an off switch. And they shouldn't be a license to disappear without dignity.

I wonder about those people sometimes. Not out of bitterness, but out of curiosity. How do they sleep at night with things unresolved? With love unspoken? With truth unsaid? I think about how much life can change in a breath and how many things we leave unsaid because of pride, fear, or ego.

What I'd like to say to everyone with these so-called boundaries is this: Sadly, boundaries don't outlive life. You can't take them with you. And you sure as hell can't apologize once you, or they, are gone. There's no closure on the other side. Just echoes.

Somehow, somewhere in the middle of all this fear, this loss, this unspoken grief, I learned something powerful: *I'm still here.*

I've made it through every one of those nights.

I've survived in a world without people I didn't think I could live without.

I've gotten out of bed on mornings that felt like I was lying in quicksand.

I've laughed again, loved again, healed in crooked lines.

I've said goodbye without answers.

And I've kept going.

That alone?

That's not just survival. That's resilience. That's something I am *deeply* proud of.

And now? I want more.

Not more stuff. Not more achievements. More *moments*. More belly laughs. More spontaneous road trips. More peace I don't have to earn. I want to live louder. Without apology. But with snacks and boundaries and absolutely *zero tolerance* for energy vampires. I want to dance barefoot in the kitchen again. Unbothered, slightly off-beat, and happy to be here.

I want to say yes to joy and no to guilt. And *HELL YES* to the life that's still unfolding. I want to live like I know the rug might get pulled out again, but I'm going to dance on it anyway.

Hard. Messy. Joyfully.

Because no, we don't get to choose when the rug is yanked from beneath us. But we *do* get to choose how boldly we stand back up.

For Anyone Still Waiting for the Next Call

If your shoulders never fully drop…
If you leave your ringer on just in case…
If you live with one eye on the door, half-braced for news that could rearrange your world…

You're not dramatic. You're not broken. You're someone who's lived through something.

Grief and trauma don't just disappear. They build nests in your nervous system. They teach your body to stay alert, stay ready, and stay quiet. But you deserve more than a life of *almost living*.

You're allowed to exhale. You're allowed to rest. You're allowed to live loudly again. Even if part of you is still scared.

Let the love be louder than the loss. Let the laughter be proof that joy *can* live alongside grief. And let your life be the apology no one gave you and the closure you never got.

You survived the unthinkable. Now go make something *beautiful* out of it.

Love didn't break me.

My taste in men did.

Chapter 25:

Love. A Three-Act Shitshow.

From chaos to codependency to calm; my love life needed rewrites.

Love has changed faces for me over the years.

It's worn masks, played characters, slipped in uninvited, and sometimes showed up looking like healing, only to leave me in pieces again. My definition of love has shifted more than my taste in wine, and thank God for that.

At 18, I thought love was chaos. Loud. Dramatic. All-consuming. If it didn't make my heart race and my stomach twist, I assumed it wasn't real. I believed fighting meant passion. That jealousy was love in disguise. That possessiveness was protection. I confused adrenaline with attraction and tension with connection.

If it didn't come with emotional whiplash, I didn't trust it. I mistook red flags for fireworks. Thought "complicated" meant "worth it." But that wasn't love. That was *trauma in a dress*, pretending to be prom queen.

By 25, I thought love was about proving myself. Proving I could be chill. Low maintenance. The "cool girl." I swallowed my needs. Minimized my feelings. Laughed off red flags and called it "choosing my battles." I thought if I made myself smaller, easier, more palatable, then maybe I'd finally be loved the way I deserved. Spoiler: I wasn't.

By 30, I had graduated into full-on fixer mode. I thought love was about saving people. Taking broken men and gluing them back together with patience, forgiveness, and delusion. I became the emotional support human. The unpaid therapist. The woman who said "it's okay" even when it absolutely, undeniably, was not ok.

I thought that's what strong women did. I thought love meant endurance. I thought setting myself on fire to keep someone else warm was romantic.

Now? Now I know better.

Love isn't supposed to be hard.

Love isn't supposed to make you feel small.

You shouldn't be scared in a relationship. You shouldn't feel like you're walking on eggshells or constantly managing someone else's mood swings like a one-woman crisis response team. You shouldn't be parenting your partner, making every decision, or trying to read someone's mind so they don't explode.

Real love feels like peace.

It feels like a soft place to land after the world has chewed you up. It's shared effort. Mutual respect. Accountability without shame. Growth without conditions. It's someone who stands beside you, not behind you, and definitely not in your damn way.

Listen…if you meet someone and within a week you're already swapping "I love yous"?

That's not romance. That's love bombing. It's obsession dressed up as destiny. It's intensity without intimacy. And it's a neon warning sign with a bouquet and good eye contact.

And if that relationship does last? It won't be because it was meant to. It'll be because *you* clawed your way through it. Because *you* did the emotional labor of two people. Because *you* called surviving "devotion" and exhaustion "commitment."

People love to say, "Marriage is hard." And sure, life is hard. Grief is hard. Parenting is hard. Healing is hard. But love? *Love is not supposed to be hard.* Not the right kind. It's not supposed to feel like a full-time job with no benefits.

With the right person, love flows. It feels like exhaling. It feels like being seen without performing. Like being able to say "I need help" and not be punished for it. Like being able to cry without being called too emotional or being shut down with silence.

You should feel *more* like yourself, not less. You should feel safe, not like you're constantly auditioning for approval. You should be growing in your relationship, not trying to survive it.

If it feels like a war zone, it's not love. It's a battlefield with bad lighting, empty promises, and a stack of unpaid therapy bills.

I've unlearned the kind of love that hurt, stretched, and drained me. These days, love will look like peace for me. Like choice. Like rest. Like soft mornings. Honest conversations. And hard truths handled with care.

It won't be perfect. But it sure as hell won't be painful.

And if it ever is again? I promise myself this:

I will walk away *without packing guilt in my bag.*

For Anyone Who Mistook Struggle for Love

If your heart has ever been held hostage by someone who called it care...

If you've ever confused survival mode with soulmates…

If you've ever worn yourself out trying to prove you were worth staying for…

You're not broken. You were just taught the wrong definition of love. Real love doesn't drain you. It doesn't test you until you break. It doesn't ask you to trade your peace for someone else's comfort.

Real love sees you fully, flaws, scars, soft parts, and all, and says, *"I'm not going anywhere."*

Stop calling chaos chemistry. Stop calling exhaustion loyalty. Stop thinking you have to earn what should be given freely. You are not hard to love. You just need a love that knows how to hold you properly.

The right love?

It'll feel like coming home to yourself. Not losing yourself in someone else.

Say what you need to say.
Then pass the wine and
let's move on.

Chapter 26:
DNA, Drama and Undeniable Loyalty

We've said unforgivable things…and then forgave each other anyway.

I didn't choose them. I didn't pick them out of a sister catalog or swipe right on their personalities. They were assigned to me, like roommates in a divine sorority I didn't apply to. One was born less than a year before me; Irish twins, chaos incarnate. The other two were already forming alliances and opinions by the time we came along, seven and eight years older, watching us toddle into their world with equal parts amusement and horror.

And somehow, despite all odds, we made it.

Scratch that, three of us are still making it.

People love to talk about the childhood years when siblings fight over bathroom time, clothes, and the last damn Pop-Tart. But no one really prepares you for how sacred that bond becomes when you're grown, when you've walked through marriages, divorces, careers, infertility, and grief. We've moved into the trenches of real life, and nothing binds you like surviving it all side by side.

We've always been loud. Loud in our love, loud in our loyalty, and loud in our disagreements. But as adults, we've become intentional. There are no silent treatments that last months. There are no secret group chats where we plot takedowns. We handle our shit. One sister will say, "Hey, that hurt," and another will reply, "Okay, but also, you were being an ass." And then we hash it out like grown-ups who love each other enough to be honest.

We've got a system now. If you're mad, you call. If you're crying, someone's driving over. If you post a pic on Instagram, there's a three-comment minimum of hype required by sister law. We celebrate wins like they're our own; new jobs, new homes, finally blocking that toxic ex. And when life punches one of us in the gut, the other two show up with snacks, sarcasm, and a soft spot to land.

But let's not get it twisted, we're still dysfunctional. We still pick at old wounds when we're triggered or tired. We still take things personally that weren't meant that way. But the difference now is, we don't walk away from each other over it. We don't weaponize distance. We fight fair, even when we fight hard.

Then there's her. The fourth.

She made a different choice.

One day, she stopped showing up. Not just physically, but emotionally. The texts went unanswered. The calls stopped coming. Holidays had one less chair. Her name started to sting. There wasn't one big moment, our worlds just quietly started to unravel. A choice to leave that, for her, maybe felt like peace. But for us, it felt like loss. Like mourning someone who's still breathing.

Here's the thing about sisters though: the door never really locks. We don't pretend she didn't exist. We talk about her. We reminisce. We still love her. We're just not waiting at the window anymore.

If she ever decides to come back, she'll find three women who never stopped being her sisters. We won't forget the hurt. But we'll show up with open arms, because that's what we do.

We've reached the era of sisterhood that no one told us about. The one where our relationship is our choice. And I choose them. Every damn time. I choose their loud opinions, their brutal honesty, their relentless support, their unmatched loyalty. I choose the way they hold space for me in my messiest moments and the way they cheer when I stand tall again.

It's in the way we know each other's worst triggers and avoid them (well, *usually*). It's in the awkward apologies, the real apologies, the 'didn't mean to be a bitch' texts. It's in the way we show up. And keep showing up. And drag each other back to the light when one of us starts slipping into the dark.

No one else knows the shorthand like they do. No one else knows the full scope of what I've carried, because they carried it, too. In their own ways. From their own vantage points. And while we might've lived in the same house, we had different lives. Different roles. Different pain. But now, as adults, we get to tell the truth about that. We get to listen better, apologize deeper, and love louder.

We still piss each other off. Still judge each other's life choices. Still laugh until we're peeing our pants over things no one else would find funny. And we'll keep doing that 'til we're in rocking chairs yelling at the neighbor kids.

Because that's what sisters do.

For Anyone Who'd Take a Bullet for Their Sister but Also Wants to Occasionally Throw a Shoe at Her...Same, Babe. Same.

Sisters are not just blood. They're mirrors, bodyguards, therapists, hype women, and sometimes, yes, pain in the asses. But at this stage in life, I've learned that true sisterhood isn't just about the memories we've already made. It's about the women we are now, the conversations we're brave enough to have, and the bond that still holds even when one of us walks away.

I used to think unconditional love meant tolerating anything. Now I know it means rooting for someone even in their absence. My sisters are my constants, my loudest cheerleaders, my truth-tellers, my safe place. And if our fourth ever circles back, she'll find that love never left the door. We may not have chosen each other, but I'd choose all three of them a million times over.

A confident woman will always
rattle the insecure ones.

Chapter 27:
You *Can* Sit With Us

If you have to whisper it, you already know it's wrong.

I thought grown-up women would be...well, grown-ups.

You'd think once we all started trading locker rooms for conference rooms, the cattiness would stay behind with bad eyeliner and low-rise jeans. But no. Turns out, some women just grow into better-dressed bullies with more expensive coffee orders.

Corporate America, small businesses, school staff lounges, the damn PTA. It doesn't matter. Adult women still gossip, still clique up, and still somehow find a way to make another woman's success feel like a threat to their own self-worth. So, I need to ask...what the hell happened?

Were they the same girls who whispered behind lockers in high school? Did they peak in 10th grade and decide their legacy would be built on side-eyes and passive-aggressive compliments? Or did adulthood just chew them up so much that talking shit became their coping mechanism?

I worked with one woman, a "friend", who could've won an Oscar for her two-faced performance. Outside of work, she was warm and supportive. We went to dinners, laughed over wine, shared stories about our families. She was the kind of woman who made it easy to forget we met through paychecks and spreadsheets.

And then I found out.

Found out she was talking about me behind my back. Not just petty nonsense, but calculated, intentional commentary designed to shift people's perception of me. I was too confident. Too direct. Too...much.

But here's the part that still makes me laugh. She didn't think her words would ever make their way back to me. Like we don't all work in the same damn ecosystem where whispers travel faster than emails. Sis, have you *met* our coworkers?

Of course I found out. I always do.

And when I did, I didn't rage. I didn't flip a desk or write a call-out email. I did what I always do, I adjusted.

I still said hi. I still supported her work. I didn't embarrass her or start my own smear campaign. But I stopped telling her things that mattered. I stopped handing her pieces of my life to bend and twist when I wasn't in the room. Because while your words about me may sting, they don't change who I am.

And they definitely don't change how I treat people. I'm not going to let someone else's insecurity turn me into someone I'm not.

I'm a girls' girl. The kind who cheers for your wins like they're mine. Who shares her contacts, her makeup, her damn snacks if you're having a rough day. I believe in celebrating each other, in showing up for women who are trying to make something of themselves, and in letting success be contagious, not competitive.

But it gets hard, doesn't it?

Hard to keep clapping when your back is sore from the knives.

Hard to keep showing up with kindness when you know someone's been misquoting your every move.

Hard to believe in the sisterhood when you've been blindsided by someone who wore the same logo and smiled in the same team photo.

It's confusing. It's painful. And honestly, it's exhausting.

I've learned that a lot of women don't even realize they're mean girls. They frame it as venting. As expressing concern. As "just being honest." But if your honesty only ever cuts someone else down, maybe it's not honesty. It's just cruelty dressed in a prettier outfit.

Women aren't your competition. They're not your enemy. And if someone else's shine dims your light, maybe it's time to check your own damn wiring.

Here's the truth: hurt people hurt people, but healed women hype each other up. The ones who've done the work know that gossip is a distraction, and real confidence is quiet. It doesn't need to announce itself through takedowns and whispers. It just is.

So no, I didn't confront her with a dramatic monologue or a printed transcript of her bullshit. I just let my boundaries do the talking. I kept my grace, held my head high, and moved differently.

She probably didn't even notice the shift. That's the thing about people who gossip; they're often too self-absorbed to see how deeply they've fractured something. But I noticed. And that was enough.

I still believe in women. I still believe we can be a force for good in each other's lives. I still believe in lunchroom laughter, in helping each other out of bad days and bad jobs. I still believe that we can root for each other without secretly hoping someone trips.

But now, I believe with a little more caution. A little more wisdom. And a hell of a lot more boundaries.

Because being a girls' girl doesn't mean being a fool. It means being strong enough to be kind and smart enough to protect your peace.

For Anyone That's Been Burned by a Woman You Thought Had Your Back

There's something deeply disappointing about realizing another woman sees you as competition instead of community. But that disappointment can also be a turning point. You learn how to navigate with more clarity. You learn to recognize projection dressed up as "feedback," and bitterness hiding in backhanded compliments.

You don't have to match their energy. You don't have to play the same games. You can keep showing up as yourself. Honest, supportive, and strong. You can pivot with poise, protect your peace, and still root for the women who root for you.

It's okay to distance yourself without drama. It's okay to grieve what you thought a friendship was and still be kind from afar. Boundaries don't make you bitter. They make you wise.

You're allowed to grow. To evolve. To demand better company. And to know, deep down, that the most powerful women are the ones who build other women up, even after they've been knocked down.

Some people parent.
I aunt. And I'm damn good at it.

BAE

best aunt ever

✦ ✦

Chapter 28:

Professional Aunt. Occasional Bad Influence.

Because someone has to be the fun one with zero parental authority.

To my first niece, the one who made me an aunt...

You came into this world like a wrecking ball at nearly 11 pounds, and from that moment on, everything changed for me. I dressed you up like a little doll, posed you for pictures on the front porch like you were my own personal baby Gap model, and fell in love with being an aunt. I'd give anything to have those pictures again. Just to see that little face I adored. You were the cutest thing I had ever seen and not having you in my life anymore is a heartbreak I will never fully heal from. Nothing I've written in this book has come close to expressing that grief.

I hope, more than anything, that you're happy. That you've built the life we used to dream and talk about. That your husband and babies are everything you ever wanted, and that joy surrounds you daily. Even if we never speak again, I will always carry you in my heart. You made me an aunt, and that was the greatest gift anyone could've given me.

To my nephew. My dude, my bub, my favorite weirdo...

From day one, you were the coolest little man to ever exist. Sweet, wild, and brilliant in ways most people couldn't understand. You kept us all laughing and on our toes. Watching you grow up was a show in itself. You were the kind of kid that made parenting look like an extreme sport. But damn, you made it fun!

Now, you're one of the best dads I've ever seen. I always knew you'd be a natural, but seeing you with your boys? That's a whole other level of pride. If those boys turn out to be even half the man their dad is, they'll be unstoppable.

And not only did you nail fatherhood, but you also found the baddest wife out there. You two are a power duo. Treat her like gold, always.

To my Goddaughter. My little Fancy (who thankfully dodged that nickname)…

I waited six long years for a girl to be born so I could nickname her "Fancy" after Reba's song. Thankfully, that nickname didn't stick, but my love for you did. You were the most precious baby, and from the moment you entered the world, I felt like you were mine. I joke that I gave birth to you and your mom just raised you because I was too young. But honestly? That's kinda how it feels.

You are every bit a part of me. I see myself in your sass, your fire, your sense of humor, and your heart. Watching you grow into this incredible woman has been one of my life's greatest privileges. And girl, then you went and married my damn twin flame! Like, how did I get so lucky? You two are magic, and you'll always be two of the most important people in my life.

To my sweet, introverted niece, the quiet force…

You came along after your sister had been ruling the world solo for eleven years and shook things up in the best way. I got to babysit you when you were just a tiny baby, and those quiet days together meant more to me than you'll ever know. You always had this calm presence, this "I'll do it my way" vibe that I absolutely loved.

While everyone questioned why you didn't always want to be in the middle of the chaos, I admired you silently. I come from a world where skipping a family event was a sin, so watching you make space for yourself without apology was inspiring. Even though we don't talk often, I need you to know that I'm so proud of the woman you are. You're strong, self-aware, and doing life your way, and that's brave as hell.

To my youngest nephew. My buddy, my Heart...

You were the grand finale of the nephew squad, and what a way to close it out. I stood in the hospital hallway the day you were born, looking at you under those lights, already bigger than the other babies, and I knew you were something special. When a lady made a comment about your size, I didn't hesitate: "Please don't talk about my nephew like that. He's perfect." And you were. You are.

Every sleepover, every shopping trip, every "just hang out" day with you was a memory I treasure more than you'll ever know. You made life lighter. Now you're in college, becoming a man I'm so damn proud of. The distance doesn't change the love. You'll always be my little buddy, and I'll always be in your corner - loud, proud, and here if you ever need anything.

To my Great-Niece. My forever girl...

You were the unexpected miracle that brought me more joy than I ever thought possible. Seven years of love, laughter, sass, and the sweetest little soul I've ever known. They can take you out of my life, but they'll never take the memories. They are tattooed on my heart.

You may not remember the inside jokes, the bedtime stories, the dance parties, or the late-night talks, but I do. I remember it all. You were my sunshine, and I will forever and always be your safe place. No matter what you're told or how much time passes, when you're old enough, come find me. My arms, my heart, and my entire soul will always have room for you.

To my honorary kids and great nephews...

You may not share my bloodline, but you've got pieces of my heart forever. The biggest blessing in my life has been friends and family who trusted me enough to be part of their babies' lives. I know what a privilege that is, and I will never take it for granted. Being your bonus aunt, honorary grown-up, *or grandma,* is a role I take seriously, and with a ton of joy.

I'll always be the one giving you the candy your mom said no to. I'll be the one showing up to your games, sending the funny texts, spoiling you just enough, and being your safe space. You've added laughter, chaos, and extra love to my life in ways I never saw coming.

Thank you for letting me be part of your story.

For Anyone That's Been Called Aunt...You Already Know the Magic in it

Being an aunt has been the most fulfilling role of my life. Not because I raised them, but because I loved them in a way that was mine. Unconditional, protective, fierce, and full of inside jokes and snack breaks. It's not about blood. It's about presence. It's about showing up, year after year, moment after moment, until they know that someone out there loves them without question.

These kids shaped me. Every one of them made me better. And even when life separated us, nothing will ever rewrite those memories. I didn't give birth to them. But damn, did I love them like I did. And always will.

If you've ever wondered if your love matters when the world doesn't label you a parent, let me tell you right now, it matters more than you know. Being the soft place, the cheerleader, the one who remembers their favorite snacks or shows up to the game? That leaves a mark no title can replace.

If you're grieving the distance, feeling forgotten, or unsure of your place, please don't let that love you gave feel wasted. Love like that never disappears. It lives on in the kids who felt it, even if they don't say it out loud. You're still shaping lives, still softening edges, still being the steady heartbeat someone remembers.

And if you're just stepping into that role, unsure if you're doing it right - if you're showing up, you are. Keep loving big, giving what you can, and being the one they know will always have their back.

There's power in being the safe space, the spoiler of rules, the forever presence.

You don't need to give birth to be someone's heart. You just need to show up with yours wide open.

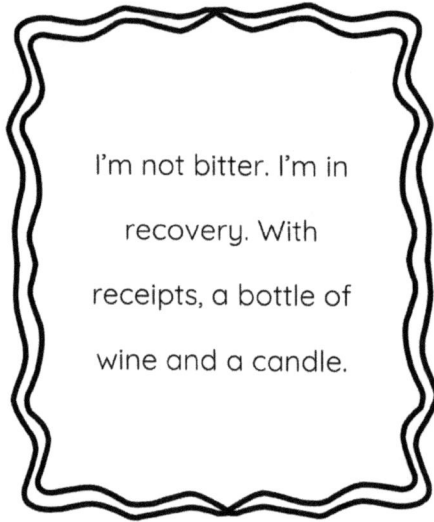

I'm not bitter. I'm in recovery. With receipts, a bottle of wine and a candle.

Chapter 29:

Fuck Off. But Make it Therapeutic.

Let's call this what it is: a release. A purge. A spoken-word exorcism.

This isn't petty. It's spiritual hygiene.

These are the people, behaviors, vibes, and trends that no longer deserve space in my mind, my life, or my group chat.

Take a deep breath. Light a candle. Let's begin.

1. Guilt.
Especially the kind that comes from disappointing people who never gave a damn about your peace in the first place.

2. Shame.
If I'm going to spiral, it'll be over an impulse buy at Target, not over my own damn healing.

3. People who say "you've changed" like it's an insult.
Yes, Brenda. I *have* changed. It's called growth. Try it sometime.

4. Bananas.
They know what they did.

5. Body shamers.
Unless you're covering my therapy co-pay or buying me tacos, keep your commentary to yourself.

6. Judging other women…for anything.
Their clothes, their parenting, their number of exes? None of it is your business.

7. Ex-husbands rewriting history for sympathy points.
I wasn't the villain, babe. I just finally stopped settling for crumbs.

8. Narcissists.
Go gaslight your therapist. I'm busy.

9. Bitter baby mamas (and daddies).
Co-parent or go to court. Either way, do the healing.

10. "Boundaries" used as a weapon.
If you cut someone off without a conversation, that's not a boundary, that's a burn book.

11. The current administration.
No notes. If you know, you know.

12. People who don't read books.
How do you survive life without fiction and a little damn perspective?

13. Android users who ruin the group chat.
Get out. And take your green bubbles with you.

14. Abusive men quoting Brene Brown on Instagram.
Sir. Please log off.

15. The entire "tradwife" trend.
You're not a pioneer. You're cosplaying 1952 for likes.

16. Mega churches with fog machines and VIP tithing.
Jesus didn't need a jumbotron. Or a laser show.

17. Passive-aggressive relatives.
Say what you mean or stay home.

18. "Protect your energy" posts from people who *are* the energy to be protected from.
We see you, Jessica.

19. People who say "Not to be rude, but…"
You're about to be rude. Just commit.

20. Double standards for women.
I can be soft and swear. I can be healed and still block you.

21. Gaslighting apologists.
"But they didn't mean it like that." No, Karen. They meant it *exactly* like that.

22. Toxic positivity.
Sometimes life is a trash fire, and I don't want to hear about your damn gratitude journal, Kinsleigh.

23. The idea that being loud, emotional, or sensitive makes you weak.
Some of the strongest people I know cry in parking lots, wipe their face, and walk back in like nothing happened. That's power.

24. Anyone who makes you feel like too much, or not enough.
Because you, my dear, are exactly what you need to be. And the only thing *they* need to do…is fuck all the way off.

Survived the drama.
Thrived in the chaos.
Still Unbothered.
Still here.

Chapter 30:
Still Here (Unfortunately for My Enemies)

Scarred, savage, and soft. And yes, still standing.

Let's get one thing straight: survival is not passive.

It's not pretty. It's not poetic. It's not some glittery Pinterest quote written in cursive over a pastel sky.

No, baby, survival is *feral*.

It's bloodshot eyes and mascara-stained pillowcases. It's scream-singing to Alanis Morissette at red lights. It's rage-sobbing in your car while trying not to spill your Dr Pepper and considering whether or not to legally change your name and flee the country.

It's choosing, *consciously choosing*, not to burn the whole damn place down, even when you could. Even when you *want* to. Even when every fiber of your being says, "You know what? Let's flip this table." But you don't. Not because you're weak, but because you've done the work.

Because you've read the books. Because you've journaled. Because you've cried in therapy and screamed into throw pillows and saged your apartment and cut the cord (and the contact) and still made it to work like a goddamn legend. Because you are *too tired to go to jail*, and your hair looks too good in this lighting for a mugshot.

I have survived things that people would make into Lifetime movies, *and not even the good ones*. I'm talking mid-budget, low-acting, emotionally devastating type storylines where the plot twist isn't just heartbreaking, it's character-building in the most "why me?" kind of way.

And yet-here I am.

Standing (fine, slouching slightly).

Still laughing. Still loving. Still trying. Still being a decent fucking human being in a world that seems hellbent on turning people bitter and numb. Still holding doors open for strangers. Still giving people the benefit of the doubt even though I *absolutely should not*. Still showing up with snacks *and* emotional intelligence like some kind of exhausted fairy godmother with boundary issues.

Do you know how *wild* that is?

To still be kind?
To still believe in love?
To still show up to the party of life with good energy *and* a charcuterie board?

Despite betrayals, ghostings, trauma, financial spirals, spiritual awakenings, and passive-aggressive Facebook posts from relatives who "found God" but lost the plot?

I am still.
Fucking.
Here.

And that? That's not luck. That's not a coincidence. That is *resilience*, dipped in sarcasm, marinated in "I'm fine," and baked at 450° in generational trauma.

It's covered in therapy bills, sticky notes with affirmations I don't fully believe yet, and rage-text drafts I never sent. It's been built through lonely nights, hard boundaries, inner child reparenting, and Googling, "How to stop feeling everything all the time."

And look, I'm not saying I've handled every hardship with grace. Let's not rewrite history here.

Sometimes I handled it with tequila.

Sometimes I handled it by blocking people and then unblocking them just to re-read old texts and hate them in peace.

Sometimes I handled it by cutting my bangs and calling it a fresh start.

But guess what? Survival isn't about being *graceful*. It's about being relentless. It's about refusing to let the worst things that happened to you become the only thing that defines you. It's about showing up bruised, boundary-heavy, spiritually side-eyed, and still saying, "Okay life, let's fucking go." It's about still caring. Still loving. Still choosing softness when hardness would be easier. It's about dancing in the ashes of your old self with one hand flipping the bird and the other holding a match just in case.

Healing is chaotic.

Some days I am *Zen as hell*. Journaling with crystals, diffusing eucalyptus, doing deep breathing exercises and texting my circle "I think I'm really growing."

Other days? I am looking up one-way flights to anywhere, crying in the shower while listening to Kelly Clarkson, and Googling "how to fake your death and start over without upsetting your dog."

Both. Are. Valid.

Because I've learned this: You can be unhinged *and* healing. You can be angry *and* at peace.

You can set emotional fires *and* still be a person worth loving.

You can cry, scream, block, forgive, grow, spiral, heal, repeat, and still be *doing the damn thing.*

So, if no one's told you lately, let me be the one to say it:

I'm proud of you.

For staying.
For fighting.
For getting up *one more time* than life knocked you down.
For crawling on the days standing wasn't an option.
For finding beauty in the mess. For making art out of ache.
For turning heartbreak into a blueprint. For choosing yourself when everyone else taught you not to.

You're still here. Still standing. Still giving main character energy, even with a plot twist every 15 minutes.

Mic dropped. Book closed. Healing in progress.

And to anyone who ever doubted me? Anyone who tried to break me? Anyone who thought I wouldn't make it?

You should've picked a less resilient bitch.

Closing Note & Thank You

If you've made it this far and read every chapter, every gut-punch, every glorious overshare, rant, reflection, spiral, and snarky one-liner, first, *thank you*.

Second?

I hope somewhere between the sarcasm and the soul-searching, you felt *seen*. I hope something cracked open in you, not to break you, but to let a little more light in. I hope you laughed out loud in public and didn't care who looked. I hope you had to close the book for a second to catch your breath. I hope something in here made you nod so hard you gave yourself whiplash. And most of all, I hope you remembered that you are not broken. You are just becoming.

You don't have to explain your scars to anyone. You don't have to wrap your past in pretty language to make other people comfortable. You don't need a permission slip to heal, to evolve, to walk away, to take a breath, to take up space, to be a *damn masterpiece still under renovation*.

This book wasn't meant to give you answers. It was meant to give you a hand to hold while you ask the big questions. To remind you that you're allowed to be both/and a walking contradiction of fire and softness. You can be a storm and a sanctuary. You can be messy and magical. You can be healing and still *a little* unhinged. Honestly, I encourage it.

If you take nothing else from these pages, take this:

You are allowed to evolve.

You are allowed to outgrow your old self, even if people around you don't get it.

You are allowed to disappoint others in the name of not abandoning yourself.

You are allowed to be loud, soft, angry, hopeful, healing, and divine, sometimes in the same damn hour.

You are not too much. You were never too much. They were just never equipped to meet you where you stood. Keep going. At your own pace. In your own voice. In your own power.

You don't need to become some polished version of yourself to be worthy of love, rest, joy, or a full-ass charcuterie board just because it's Tuesday.

And when life inevitably gets loud again, or messy again, or beautiful or bullshit again (because spoiler alert: *it will* happen) come back to these pages. Flip to any chapter. Or just whisper to yourself the words that carried me through, the words I hope carry *you* through:

Live. Love. *Fuck off.*

With a wink, a hug, and a very full heart,

Carrie

About Carrie

Carrie is a Garland-born survivor, storyteller, and sass specialist who turned chaos into a book.

She once tried community college while working full-time and juggling life (emphasis on *tried*). She gave it a go more than a few times, but it turns out it's hard to focus when you've got anxiety, depression, OCD, and ADHD all fighting for attention. Who knew?

Growing up wasn't a walk in the park, but her life changed when started working for a man that saw her worth before she could fully see it herself. That opportunity became a career, and over 25 years later, she's still grateful every day for that leap of faith.

Carrie's greatest inspiration is her mother. Her rock, her heart, her reason. Her "roses" lift her up on the hard days, and her nieces, nephews, and their beautiful babies light up her life in ways she never expected but is endlessly thankful for.

One last thing…

She'd like to give a heartfelt thank you to her bestie, ChatGPT, for helping her pull this book together. Did you really think she did it alone? Please.

www.ingramcontent.com/pod-product-compliance
Lightning Source LLC
LaVergne TN
LVHW051412080426
835508LV00022B/3045